DEFINING MOMENTS

DEFINING MOMENTS

Historic Decisions by Arkansas Governors from McMath through Huckabee

ROBERT L. BROWN

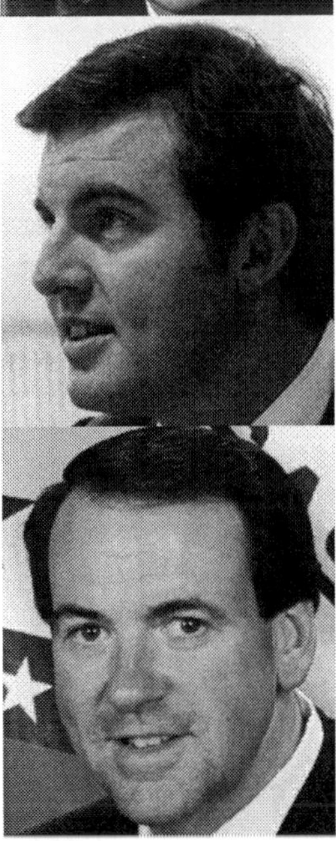

The University of Arkansas Press
Fayetteville
2010

Manufactured in the United States of America

ISBN-10: 1-55728-944-1
ISBN-13: 978-1-55728-944-5

14 13 12 11 10 6 5 4 3 2

Designed by Liz Lester

∞ The paper used in this publication meets the minimum requirements of the American National Standard for Permanence of Paper for Printed Library Materials Z39.48-1984.

LIBRARY OF CONGRESS CATALOGING-IN-PUBLICATION DATA

Brown, Robert L., 1941–
Defining moments: Historic decisions by Arkansas governors from McMath through Huckabee / Robert L. Brown.
p. cm.
Includes bibliographical references.
ISBN-13: 978-1-55728-944-5 (cloth : alk. paper)
ISBN-10: 1-55728-944-1 (cloth : alk. paper)
1. Arkansas—Politics and government—1951–
2. Governors—Arkansas—History. I. Title.
F415.B76 2010
976.7'053—dc22
2010022652

Cover images: McMath, Cherry, Faubus, Rockefeller, Pryor, Clinton photos courtesy of the Butler Center Photos at the Arkansas Studies Institute; Bumpers photo courtesy of the Arkansas History Commission collection; White photo courtesy of Gay White; Tucker photo courtesy of Special Collections, University of Arkansas, Fayetteville; Huckabee photo courtesy of the Ouachita Baptist University Special Library Collection

To Charlotte

CONTENTS

ACKNOWLEDGMENTS

My personal thanks to Martha Patton, who took this project on as a second job and worked nights and weekends on multiple drafts, often catching my mistakes. My thanks, too, to Martha F. Ferson, a student at the University of the South (Sewanee), and Brian Pipkin, who labored mightily at the History Commission researching spools of Arkansas newspapers. Megan Hargraves also filled the role of spot researcher as did Jennifer Flinn.

Rod Miller at the Supreme Court Library was more than willing to find what was available at his library and to cast a wide net to discover what might be available at the Arkansas Legislative Research Office and the History Commission as well as the State Library. Elizabeth Danley, senior reference librarian at the State Library, was especially helpful, as was Cheryl Reinhart at the Legislative Research Office.

Keith Melton at the Arkansas Arts Center was an immeasurable help in garnering relevant George Fisher cartoons. Linda Pine and Jennifer McCarty at the University of Arkansas at Little Rock library filled a similar role for Jon Kennedy cartoons and in finding helpful pictures of the governors.

Other pictures of the governors were provided through Tom Dillard, director of the University of Arkansas Library at Fayetteville, and Geoffery Stark of the special library collection; Lyn Eubanks of the History Commission; Brian Robertson of the Institute of Arkansas Studies; Barry Arthur and Frank Fellone of the *Arkansas Democrat-Gazette;* and Ray Granade of Ouchita Baptist University Library.

I am indebted to each and every one of these people for their willing assistance.

FOREWORD

The journalist Mignon McLaughlin once observed that "courage can't see around corners, but goes around them anyway." In many respects, that's what this wonderful book is all about: the courage and convictions of men in positions of enormous responsibility, when faced with decisions that had the potential to imperil their political careers.

With the objectivity and intellect of a supreme court justice, the scholarship of a political historian, the engaging style of a professional storyteller, and the familiarity of a friend, Bob Brown crystallizes the difficult choices faced by ten former Arkansas governors. He shows how their decisions at crucial points not only defined those moments but shaped their tenures, shaped their legacies, and sometimes even shaped history.

In areas from education to the environment, social justice to the conduct of politics, Arkansas governors have grappled with many of our nation's defining debates. For Sid McMath, the question was whether or not to support President Harry Truman's civil rights platform against the Dixiecrat tide. In the 1950s, Francis Cherry faced the temptation of tarring his campaign rival as a Communist. Orval Faubus's role in the desegregation of Little Rock Central High has become part of America's civil rights history. In the turbulent days after Martin Luther King's assassination, Winthrop Rockefeller's public posture would affect the course of Arkansas race relations.

Dale Bumpers confronted a redistricting dilemma that represented the old ways versus the "new politics" in Arkansas. For David Pryor, the decisive issue concerned the environment: a dam on the Strawberry River. Frank White put himself at the center of a debate about the role of religion in schools. Bill Clinton took on the challenge of teacher testing—a subject that remains central to our nation's educational reform efforts. Jim Guy Tucker faced his defining moment in a special legislative session to close a Medicaid financing gap. And the controversial question of consolidating public school districts offered Mike Huckabee an opportunity to prove his mettle and his vision.

I've been privileged to know and work with many of these men myself—including meeting Orval Faubus when I was elected governor as a high school student at Boys State; knowing Jim Guy Tucker, beginning with our days together as students at the University of Arkansas; working with Governor Winthrop Rockefeller when I was student body president at the University of Arkansas; serving in the legislature in my early twenties, during Governor Dale Bumpers's first term; supporting Frank White when he chaired the Arkansas Industrial Development Commission under Governor David Pryor, for whom I'd been campaign treasurer; also serving as treasurer of Bill Clinton's campaign and eventually following him all the way to White House; and hailing from the same hometown as President Clinton and Governor Mike Huckabee as well.

Foreshadowing it all, I actually met two of these men on the very same day, when I was ten years old. Francis Cherry was running for the Arkansas House, and David Pryor was driving him around, and they came to my parents' house in Hope so Candidate Cherry could visit with my father. I was much more interested in the candidate's driver—an All-District Camden Panther Quarterback—than in talking to a future governor. Little did I know the football star was a future governor too!

I'm struck and humbled by the number of extraordinarily talented national leaders my small state has produced, including a string of charismatic, capable, progressive Arkansan governors who set the tone for Arkansas and the South. With these profiles and vignettes, Justice Brown has assembled a lesson-book on leadership and the difficulties of decision-making in the moments it matters most. Some of the men involved were overwhelmed, or fell victim to ambition. The majority found the courage not only to handle things right, but also to do the right thing.

MACK MCLARTY

PROLOGUE

Once to Every Man and Nation, comes the Moment to Decide.

—JAMES RUSSELL LOWELL

The idea of examining a defining moment for each of Arkansas's governors over the past sixty years has always intrigued me. I first thought of it in terms of John F. Kennedy's Pulitzer prize–winning book, *Profiles in Courage.* The evolution of that concept over the years, having mulled it over and massaged the idea, has been to expand the notion to include moments when a governor was confronted with a significant decision with severe political ramifications and made his choice, rightly or wrongly. History, of course, will be the judge of that. But the true mettle of us all is best determined by how we deal with an issue that threatens our security, political or otherwise. In the case of this state's governors, the issue would be one, as conventional wisdom would have it, that might well jeopardize and even "sink" that governor's political career.

Arkansas is renowned as a state which is small enough where "everyone knows everyone," and because of this we know our politicians, and particularly our governors, personally. It is a rare individual who has not shaken Bill Clinton's hand at least once or, more often than not, multiple times. The same holds for Dale Bumpers and David Pryor and, in recent years, Jim Guy Tucker, Mike Huckabee, and Mike Beebe. Because of this, I have known the men I write about, at least casually. I worked for two of them as an aide (Dale Bumpers and Jim Guy Tucker) and supported two others (Winthrop Rockefeller and Bill Clinton) either by precinct work or monetarily. My firsthand experience as well as observation and my love for politics and public service make this subject uniquely appealing to me.

Arkansas has been blessed, in these past six decades, with a string of uniquely qualified and accomplished governors and a few governors who held great promise but saw their ship ultimately founder when the moment of truth arrived. Few states can claim the likes of a Rockefeller, a president of the United States, and several presidential contenders and a favorite-son candidate in such a brief period of time, as can Arkansas. This all proves the point that the caliber of our state executives, by and large, has been very high indeed.

A word needs to be said about courage and, in this case, political courage. The word *courage* derives from thc Latinate word for heart. I am convinced that it is a good heart that leads most men and women into public service and ultimately to the governor's seat. (Dale Bumpers and Governor Mike Beebe call public service and politics a noble calling, as did John F. Kennedy before them.) But it is an even greater heart that is willing to risk sacrificing the honor, power, and prestige of the job for what is right, honorable, and good. That is what this book seeks to explore—men who did just that (all of Arkansas's governors have been men) and those who flinched in the face of controversy or in other ways allowed their personal beliefs to blur their vision and judgment.

In some instances, I employ my imagination and concoct a dialogue of the principals or enter into their minds to support my understanding of the events that transpired. Obviously, I was not present at some of these events, armed with a recorder, but I have no doubt that the reenactments I have framed are reasonable depictions of what occurred.

DEFINING MOMENTS

Sid McMath as governor. *Courtesy of Butler Center photos, Arkansas Studies Institute Collection, Little Rock.*

SID MCMATH
1949–1953

It Matters Not How Straight the Gate
How Charged with Punishments the Scroll.
I am the Master of My Fate
I am the Captain of my Soul.

—"INVICTUS," W. E. HENLEY

On February 2, 1948, President Harry Truman issued his civil rights message to Congress. He wrote: "Not all groups are free to live and work where they please or to improve their conditions of life by their own efforts. Not all groups enjoy the full privileges of citizenship."[1] He called on Congress to enact "modern, comprehensive civil rights laws, adequate to the needs of the day, and demonstrating our continuing faith in the free way of life."[2]

Then Truman got specific. What particularly grated on him were the stories that black veterans had returned from serving their country in World War II and were immediately subjected to brutal beatings and other abuse in the South. He advocated federal law against "the crime of lynching, against which I cannot speak too strongly."[3] He urged the elimination of the poll tax, an end to segregation in interstate travel, and fair and equal job opportunities for blacks.

Truman's civil rights message immediately became anathema in the South. U.S. senator Harry Byrd of Virginia warned of bloodshed.[4] U.S. senator James Eastland of Mississippi said Truman was trying to "mongrelize the south."[5] U.S. senators and their wives boycotted the Democratic Party's Jefferson-Jackson Day fundraiser at the Mayflower Hotel in Washington, D.C., the same month Truman gave his message to Congress. At the annual Democratic Convention in Little Rock, over half of the guests left when toastmaster R. A. "Brick" Lile announced that President Truman's radio address would be broadcast to the convention and that the delegates owed the president the courtesy of listening. The seeds of the Dixiecrat rebellion against Truman had been sown.

The leader of the anti-Truman forces in Arkansas was no less a person than the sitting governor, Ben Laney. Petitions were being circulated against Truman because of his civil rights stand and were given to Laney, who expressed his hate-Truman sentiment to the Democratic Party leadership in no uncertain terms. He would soon become chairman of the Arkansas States Rights Democrats, which was the formal name for the Dixiecrats. In truth, the Dixiecrats had one plank in their party platform—opposition to Truman's civil rights message. A cheap black workforce maintained under a segregated system was essential to the agrarian economy in the Mississippi Delta. Not surprisingly, this part of the state was the stronghold of the Dixiecrats. With his civil rights proposals, President Truman had thrown down the gauntlet and challenged the South.

Sid McMath wanted to be governor of Arkansas more than life itself, and he knew that the goal was well within his reach. He had earned his stripes as a hard-charging prosecutor and as part of the G. I. Revolt that had taken on the corrupt political machine in seemy Hot Springs and, specifically, Mayor Leo McLaughlin, who embodied the corruption. Yet his close friends and advisors in June 1948 were worried. The reason was simple. The newly formed Dixiecrat party had endorsed South Carolina governor Strom Thurmond as its presidential candidate to oppose Truman and was putting inordinate pressure on gubernatorial aspirant McMath to join its ranks.

For advice, McMath focused particularly on his campaign manager and strategist, former FBI agent Henry Woods from Texarkana. Three decades later, Woods would be appointed federal district judge for the Eastern District of Arkansas, but in 1948, he was known primarily for his love of politics and as the former state president of the Young Democrats.

Woods would lean back in his chair and puff on his ubiquitous cigar. Then he would put down the cigar, clasp his hands behind his head, and begin to speak in the Texarkana twang that was his trademark. McMath knew that though Woods tended toward pontification and prolixity, his analysis was always razor sharp. Woods had laid out the clashing points of view and ended with a brutally frank assessment of what endorsing Truman would mean to a McMath candidacy. He concluded that it could prove costly. Woods noted in particular that McMath's principal foe in the democratic primary for governor would be former state attorney general Jack Holt, who, though not an announced Dixiecrat, tilted to the segregationist point of view. No matter how you cut it, race would be the pivotal issue in the campaign.

There was an inherent conflict in Sid McMath, as there was in many southerners of that time. He was the product of the Civil War, General Robert E. Lee having only surrendered his Confederate army at Appomattox Courthouse eighty-three years earlier. Many of his forebears, including two grandfathers (Edgar Sanders and James Rudd), had fought as Confederates, and he grew up reveling in their stories. Like most southerners, he revered Robert E. Lee and described him as the "epitome of character."[6] The South, he knew, had been bloodied as much by Reconstruction and its aftermath as by the war. One quarter of the South's men had been killed or wounded in the war, and its land and wealth had been pillaged.[7] Even in the 1940s, onerous tariffs and fees assessed by Congress continued to hold the South hostage. McMath knew this for a fact—he had lived it—and at one level he was bitter because of it.

But at another level, he recoiled at the inhumanity of slavery and the brutality of the sharecropping and leased-prisoner systems that continued long after the Civil War to keep African Americans enslaved. At an early age, he witnessed the whipping of an African American male, and it seared his mind forever. He vowed, "Someday, some way, I would help these people."[8] Having black friends as a young boy cemented this commitment.

Sid McMath, at age thirty-six, was now entering the race of his life, and he recognized the tantalizing expediency of the Dixiecrat cause. States' rights still was a rallying cry in much of Arkansas, and demagoguery on race had "sold" well in the past in the hands of such flamboyant and unscrupulous figures as Governor Jeff Davis. At the same time, McMath knew Arkansas was changing in its attitudes toward race. World War II and an emerging economy had much to do with it. He also knew that part of the state, the mountainous northwest, had initially balked at secession from the Union before the Civil War and that people there had never viewed race with the intensity of their Mississippi Delta counterparts.

For most sprouting politicians of the post–World War II era, the dilemma presented by the Dixiecrats caused much anguish and consternation. Race, after all, was the acknowledged third rail in southern politics, and openly associating with the cause of equal rights for African Americans was political death. The question, though, was whether to embrace, even tacitly, the segregationist position of the Dixiecrats, which was overtly hostile to black civil rights, or to support President Truman. Sid McMath had to choose.

By his own account, McMath, born in 1912, spent much of his first ten years in a two-room "dogtrot" log cabin on the McMath home place in Columbia County, so named because the dogs could trot between the two rooms through an open air passageway.[9] It was a time before central plumbing, electricity, or paved roads. Hal McMath, his father, was of Scottish ancestry and preferred horse trading to farming cotton. He was also a problem drinker with a Mr. Hyde temperament when he went on his regular benders. The signs that the wheels were about to come off were always there, according to grandson Phillip McMath. He would buy a white Stetson hat and ride off to town.[10] The McMath family existed, hand to mouth, and moved around south Arkansas looking for a better life. McMath's mother, Nettie Belle Sanders, and both his paternal and maternal grandmothers were pillars of support. The refrain voiced by many hardscrabble cotton farmers resonated with the McMaths: "Ten-cent cotton and forty-cent meat, how in the world can a poor man eat?"[11]

Though McMath was reluctant to talk about his mother, Nellie Belle was his rock and foundation. The bond between the two was complete, and she fostered in him his sensitivity to the plight of African Americans, in contrast to his father, who was a rabid segregationist. It was she who could not bear the suffering and debasement wrought by segregation, and she poured the seeds of her Methodist values into her young son, where they took root and flourished.

When he was ten, the family moved first to Smackover and then to Hot Springs, where young Sid put his innate salesmanship to work with such wares as hot dogs, soda pop, and newspapers. He joined the Boy Scouts, which nurtured his yearning for discipline and regimen. He boxed to earn cash. He developed a fondness for acting and oratory, which later would stand him in good stead on the political hustings. He liked poetry and had a repertoire of memorized poems which he would use to regale and court young women.

The rest of his story is stuff for a Hollywood script. He was elected president of the student body at the University of Arkansas. He married his childhood sweetheart, Elaine Broughton, and they had a son, Sandy. Sadly, Elaine died after five years of marriage. He fought in the Pacific Theater as a commissioned marine and was awarded the Silver Star and Legion of Honor for valor in the Bougainville Campaign in the Solomon Islands. He mustered out as a lieutenant colonel and returned to Hot Springs to practice law.

McMath was all grit and gristle with matinee-idol looks and a twinkle in his eye. He exuded toughness and inspired confidence. He was the perfect candidate for the brave new world of hope and optimism that abounded after World War II. He chose a new partner in marriage, Anne Phillips of Mississippi.[12]

Quickly, he and a group of veterans formed the G. I. Revolt to take on the entrenched political machine in Hot Springs led by Mayor McLaughlin. Other veterans across the country were also entering political life, most notably future president John F. Kennedy in Boston, Massachusetts. McMath won the race for prosecuting attorney as part of the G. I. Revolt and successfully

Sid McMath exhibiting his Hollywood charisma. *Courtesy of Butler Center photos, Arkansas Studies Institute Collection, Little Rock.*

attacked voting fraud and political corruption, which were endemic in Hot Springs.

That was 1946. Now, two years later, there was the race for governor. But instead of a campaign waged on the significant issues of roads, rural electrification, education, and medical care, the Truman civil rights address to Congress made the Dixiecrat cause a force of nature to contend with. These thoughts, no doubt, rambled through McMath's mind as he discussed strategy with campaign manager Woods. Could they keep the state in the Democrat fold? McMath knew one thing for certain. He had to be elected governor first. And if successful, he would then take on the Dixiecrats.

But even to win the governor's seat, McMath had to confront and defeat the dragon of racial bigotry, and he was already viewed suspiciously by many as "a liberal." He had nine opponents, but his two principal adversaries were Jack Holt and "Uncle Mac" McKrell. Holt, with his credentials as former attorney general and circuit judge, loomed as the primary opponent. McKrell was "a kind of roving preacher" who brought with him a gospel quartet and free sacks of flour.[13] Not surprisingly, Holt and McMath wound up in the August runoff. And race surfaced as an issue, as McMath later put it, "big time."[14]

McKrell endorsed Holt in the runoff, and McMath was bombarded with incendiary racial innuendos on radio, in the newspapers, and in campaign literature. The questions fired at McMath publicly in campaign brochures were demagogic in the extreme:

> Where do you stand on the black issue?
>
> What deals have you made with the Negroes for the Negro vote?

> How many Negroes have you promised to put on the State Department of Education?
>
> Did your campaign manager, Henry Woods, receive a letter from a Negro king-pin in Texarkana saying that you would get the Negro vote in Miller County?
>
> Did the *Arkansas State Press,* a Negro paper in Little Rock, write an editorial supporting you for governor?
>
> Did that same paper, only last Friday, carry a front page statement that you got the Negro vote, and that the Negro vote was responsible for you leading the ticket?
>
> How much money have the Negroes contributed to your campaign?[15]

The racist strategy was almost successful, but McMath won the runoff by ten thousand votes. He immediately turned his attention to the Dixiecrats.

By August, Governor Strom Thurmond of South Carolina and Governor Fielding Wright of Mississippi had been officially nominated as presidential and vice presidential candidates, respectively, by the Dixiecrat Party. And they, with the fervent support of Governor Laney, Amis Guthridge, Crossett lawyer Jim Johnson, and planter-lawyer John Daggett of Marianna, were making an all-out assault to win Arkansas to their camp. McMath would have none of it. He was a Democrat, first and foremost, who believed in Harry Truman and Roosevelt before him. And he abhorred race baiting, even when disguised under the banner of states' rights. He first refused to host Thurmond at a Marianna meeting on August 24, 1948, where strategy was being planned to capture the Arkansas electoral votes for the Dixiecrats. He refused even to attend the meeting.[16] But the Dixiecrat pressure was becoming more and more formidable.

McMath did not avoid the challenge. He knew full well that as governor-designee, he had immense political currency which he could use with undecided delegates. The Democratic Convention was to be held in September, and he had his lieutenants set about to organize the convention so that Truman delegates would win. McMath tirelessly lobbied vacillating delegates, twisting arms and making pledges, and by September 22, it seemed he would prevail. But he had not counted on a stem-winder of a speech by Governor Laney, who, according to press accounts, "castigated" Truman with "sharp words."[17] Laney called on all Southerners "to repudiate the shady, lousy, actions of the Democratic Party's leadership of the last few months."[18]

Laney had miscalculated. He did not so much persuade as anger convention delegates. The Dixiecrats quickly abandoned their fight for state delegates, and the end result was a convention that selected Truman supporters as its delegates. The Dixiecrats' effort to usurp the Democratic Party in Arkansas had gone down in flames, and the work done by Sid McMath was largely the reason. In his speech as governor-designee, he thanked the convention for preserving the Democratic Party and for "preventing discord from disrupting our ranks."[19]

The battle, however, was far from over. Governor Ben Laney was selected as chairman of the Arkansas States Rights Democrats on October 8, 1948, and Amis Guthridge was dubbed the campaign manager for the state.[20] The Dixiecrats were pulling out all the stops to carry Arkansas. A week before the election, Strom Thurmond visited Little Rock and attacked Truman's anti-poll tax, anti-segregation and anti-lynching stance, and the Fair Employment Practice measure. He sounded the alarm against a national police force and the loss of state constitutional rights.[21] The die, though, had been cast. Truman won handily in Arkansas over both Republican Thomas Dewey and Dixiecrat

Sid McMath, with President Harry Truman, parades down Main Street in Little Rock, 1949. *Courtesy of the McMath Law Firm.*

Strom Thurmond. Thurmond, however, outpolled Dewey and came in second.

Sid McMath could have sat firmly on the fence in the Dixiecrat conflict and quietly supported Truman. But that was not his nature. He agreed totally with Truman on his civil rights message, and he proved that Arkansans would not fall victim to a bigoted appeal premised on people's worst instincts.

Two days after Truman's election, McMath announced to the General Assembly that he would ask it to start the process to "kill" the poll tax, which for decades had thwarted African American voters from exercising their right to vote.[22] He would go on to support anti-lynching legislation, a comprehensive roads program, rural electrification, consolidated schools, and an expanded medical school. But his stand against the Dixiecrats was his finest moment.

Nine years after beating back the Dixiecrat movement in 1948, McMath would see it resuscitated in the hands of Orval Faubus. On September 29, 1957, McMath said in an interview with NBC's television commentator John Chancellor that "Dixiecrat elements have taken over [Faubus's] administration" and that "a third term is in the back of [Faubus's] mind."[23] The allusion was to Faubus allies Amis Guthridge and Jim Johnson, who had been at the forefront of the Arkansas Dixiecrats during Truman's candidacy.

Sid McMath's efforts were not lost on Harry Truman. Eleven days after he won reelection in 1948, Truman wrote to McMath: "It was a great victory and you may be sure that I fully realize the part you played in bringing it about."[24]

In the last years of McMath's life (he died in 2003), he was totally blind, but his memory, especially for the verse he had learned as a youth, never faltered. On one memorable occasion, this author and McMath alternated reciting lines from the poem "Invictus," which describes raw courage in the face of adversity. The poem described McMath to perfection.

Francis Cherry
1953–1955

The first duty of a politician is to be reelected.

—POLITICAL ADAGE

It was said of Warren G. Harding, the twenty-ninth president of the United States, that he looked like a president. So it was with Francis Cherry. He looked like a governor. Handsome and stately with a flowing mane of white hair and with an erect bearing reminiscent of the chancery judge he had once been, his appearance exuded probity and inspired confidence.

Cherry rode into office in the gubernatorial election of 1952 with the help of the third-term curse that had worked historically against third-term seekers like Sid McMath. Additional help was provided by the highway-bond scandal that afflicted the McMath administration in its waning days and led to allegations of pervasive corruption. Bolstered by marathon talk-a-thons on the radio, where voters called in questions, Cherry won accolades for his measured, simplistic answers and Mr. Clean image. He bested three other opponents (Boyd Tackett, Jack Holt, and Ike Murry) in the preferential primary; and in the runoff against McMath, he won by over one hundred thousand votes.[1]

Francis Cherry as governor. *Courtesy of Butler Center photos, Arkansas Studies Institute Collection, Little Rock.*

It quickly became apparent, however, that Cherry's political skills did not extend much beyond his radio talk-a-thons. As governor, his attitude toward the General Assembly in 1953 was one of standoffishness, as if he feared that the give-and-take of legislative politics would impugn his integrity. In one glaring political error, he vetoed a sales-tax exemption for seed, feed, and fertilizer after it passed the General Assembly when he had vowed to support it in his political campaign. He further alienated the General Assembly by failing to call the legislature into special session to regain some control over the state Highway Commission. This was after the people had adopted the Mack-Blackwell Amendment to the Arkansas Constitution to remove the Highway Commission from state politics.[2]

But perhaps his perceived conspiracy with the mammoth electrical powerhouse Arkansas Power and Light Company ultimately proved his undoing. During his tenure as governor, AP&L received a 13 percent rate increase while the electrical co-ops who furnished electricity to rural areas fared poorly. The fact that Cherry was believed to control the Public Service Commission, which approved the rate increase, and to be unduly influenced by AP&L, did nothing to dispel the voters' anxiety.

Cherry also boasted of removing ten thousand recipients from the welfare rolls, including aged recipients whom he called "old dead heads." This would later be bona fide political fodder for Orval Faubus, who made much of the destitute Arkansans whom Cherry had deprived of basic sustenance.

Still, after a year and a half in office, the accepted political wisdom was that Cherry was a shoe-in for a second term. There was one embryonic political figure, however, who had an uncanny sense of what people thought and believed and who did not subscribe to that conventional thought—Orval Faubus. Faubus had been closely aligned with Sid McMath as a McMath appointee to the Highway Commission and as McMath's administrative assistant. He filed for governor at the last minute against Cherry, and, with the help of two other candidates (Guy "Mutt" Jones was one of them), forced the governor, who got only 48 percent of the vote, into a run off.[3] Faubus, the unknown, who adroitly capitalized on Cherry's political weaknesses, had polled an amazing 34 percent.

Faubus had been right—Cherry was vulnerable—and now the governor was frightened. It was then that Cherry was made privy to damning information about his run-off rival by *Arkansas Recorder* publisher John Wells.[4] Faubus had attended a reputed communist school, Commonwealth College in Mena. McCarthyism, which was named for the fear-mongering surrounding the communist threat fostered by Senator Joe McCarthy of Wisconsin, was still in vogue. The issue was a combustible one, and the question was whether Francis Cherry would use it, and if so, how?

In the eyes of the Cherry camp, the Commonwealth issue was a gift that would assure his victory. The hard question, though, was who would be the messenger for the story—a third party like Texarkana prosecutor Boyd Tackett, or Cherry himself. Tackett knew the story and was primed and ready to go forward with it. But the decision was made that Cherry would do it, and Tackett was offended.[5] He ultimately joined forces with Faubus in the runoff.

Initially, Cherry was supremely uncomfortable making the Commonwealth attack, and at one point he became physically ill because of it.[6] He did, however, make the charge in a television address on August 2, and then across the state.[7] The attack quickly bore fruit, and Cherry flayed Faubus with the message at every campaign stop.

Faubus answered the charges by first saying they were fabricated. That was untrue. But then he used his homespun references for which he became famous. An example was: "I am as American as the cornbread and blackeyed peas on which I was reared. I am just as free of subversion as the spring that flows from a mountain to form the White River."[8] Cherry ultimately saw the impact of his miraculous issue begin to dissipate.

Some members of the press were deeply offended by Cherry's blatant McCarthyism. Harry Ashmore, editorial writer for the *Arkansas Gazette*, who eventually became an intransigent Faubus foe over the Central High crisis, wrote a speech for Faubus that was delivered in Pine Bluff responding to the Cherry attack.[9] The speech included this: "When I went out from the green valley of my youth . . ." Faubus particularly liked that phrase.[10] By the end of the runoff, Faubus was making jokes about the attempted smear. To a large, applauding assembly, he would say, "There sure are a lot of communists here tonight."[11]

Faubus also benefited enormously from Cherry's alienation of members of the General Assembly and his less than cordial treatment of several major political players across the state, like Maurice Smith Sr. of Cross County and Yell County sheriff Earl Ladd.[12] Those slights were not forgotten quickly. Cherry's wife, Margaret, exacerbated the problem. As an example, the story goes that she accused the governor of turning the mansion into a "political den" when she saw Guy "Mutt" Jones there after the preferential primary.[13] Jones had come to discuss endorsing Cherry in the runoff. Understandably offended, he left and immediately endorsed Faubus.

Slowly, over the two-week period preceding the runoff election, Faubus was able to put his campaign back on course and focus the electorate on his impoverished beginnings, his thirst for education—even at a Commonwealth College—and Cherry's elitism. He won the election by 6,585 votes.[14]

For the most part, Cherry's one term as governor served as an interregnum between the McMath and Faubus regimes, which shared many of the same beliefs on rural electrification, roads, and education. Perhaps Cherry's most lasting achievement was the establishment of the Department of Finance and Administration, which centralized revenue and budgetary matters into one department. His choice, however, to embrace the Red Scare as a political tactic converted him into the very type of demagogue he deplored. He prided himself on his rectitude and integrity, and yet his ambition ultimately overrode his principles. He played what should have been a devastating political hand and lost due to his overall political ineptness, an angered political establishment, and Faubus's masterful political acumen.

Orval Faubus

1955–1967

He was just a human country boy, who believed like we have always believed back here in the hills that even the plainest, poorest fellow can be Governor if his fellow citizens find he has got the stuff and the character for the job.

—ROBERT PENN WARREN,
ALL THE KING'S MEN

Orval Faubus liked being governor. He liked the power and the trappings, but most of all he liked the fact that people knew who he was. Even the swells who lived in the Heights in west Little Rock knew him now. They may have looked down on him as that hillbilly or country bumpkin from Greasy Creek in the Francis Cherry campaign, but by golly jingle they knew who he was now, and they had to deal with him.

At issue in August 1957 was race or, more specifically, the integration of Little Rock's Central High School by a plan designed by Virgil Blossom, superintendent of the Little Rock public schools. Though the number of integrating blacks had originally been much higher, it had fallen to just nine, primarily due to fear

Orval Faubus as governor. *Courtesy of Butler Center photos, Arkansas Studies Institute Collection, Little Rock.*

in the African American community—fear about lost jobs and the safety of their children. Those nine were selected because of their academic talent. The curriculum at Central High was rigorous, and the nine students in this test case had to be able to cope with the challenge.

The Blossom plan, Faubus knew, as he mulled over the editorials by Harry Ashmore in the *Arkansas Gazette*, had seemed inspired: begin by integrating only at the high school level with a few talented African American students. Then get the city leadership on board, as Blossom had done, with a multitude of civic-club speeches. The civic leaders in Little Rock, as a result, now were resigned to what was coming. They might not like it, but it was the law, and they were resigned. Faubus knew that Blossom was pleased with himself. He knew that Blossom saw his plan as a blueprint for integration across the South and perhaps even as a springboard for his own candidacy for governor.[1]

Faubus, no doubt, smiled to himself, even while his stomach twisted in knots. What the city fathers in the capital city had failed to realize was that the average citizens might not agree with Blossom or his plan or the U.S. Supreme Court, which called for desegregation of the public schools in 1954. The Supreme Court did not make laws, Faubus knew. Congress did. And Faubus believed the people knew that. He had been on the hustings in 1956 against a rabble-rousing segregationist, Jim Johnson, who stirred the pot of racial hatred like a master and with great aplomb. An increase in taxes might be an attractive issue for the ordinary demagogue, but nothing compared to racial bigotry as the means to mobilize the masses in the South. Jim Johnson had known this for years. Now Orval Faubus did.

Faubus had smoothed the editorial page of the *Arkansas Gazette* flat on the table in front of him. "Time of Testing," the editorial crowed on the front page of the *Arkansas Gazette,* as it called for law and order.[2] "What law?" he thought. "The *Brown* desegregation decision? That's not law. The *Gazette* wants integration." Yes, not even his friend Harry Ashmore, who supported him editorially in the Francis Cherry campaign and against Jim Johnson, understood the simmering hatred that needed only a spark to convert it into a boiling fury. Johnson knew how to provide that spark. Faubus had seen it firsthand. And it frightened him.

His office had received the constant telephone calls.[3] The callers had warned of violence at Central High School perpetrated by caravans of armed men driving to Little Rock to halt integration. There will be blood on the streets, the callers warned. How real were the threats? He did not know. But he had gotten the calls. And Blossom had, too.

Yes, all eyes were on Orval Faubus now. The question was what would he do?

Orval Faubus believed in education. He had been a public school teacher himself during the height of the Great Depression, teaching for forty dollars a month in the hamlets of Accident, Pinnacle, and Greasy Creek in Madison County, and he recognized that for the impoverished hillbillies, education provided the path to a better life.[4]

Though he had denied attending the suspect Commonwealth College in Mena during the recent runoff election against Francis Cherry in 1954, that statement was false. He had sought out Commonwealth College for his higher education and hitchhiked to get there. It was a school that, however you wished to dub it, socialist or communist, was decidedly radical and diametrically opposed to capitalism. While there for at least three months, he was elected president of the school and was selected to be the May Day speaker.[5] Regardless of the college's political persuasion, his attendance there for several months and his steadfast desire to be educated against tremendous economic odds revealed his appreciation for what education could do for him and for others like him. It was a way out of the hills.

A stint in county politics and service with General George Patton's Third Army in World War II toughened Faubus and enhanced his perspective. Madison County was too small for him. He campaigned for another veteran, Sid McMath, who rewarded Faubus by appointing him to the Highway Commission after McMath's successful campaign for governor. More than anyone else, McMath was his mentor. After eighteen months as highway commissioner, he became McMath's administrative assistant in the governor's office.[6]

One of his many attractions to McMath was his program for education. McMath had championed higher teacher pay and consolidated school districts and made a longer school year, all of which Faubus applauded. If anything, the election of Faubus in 1954 was viewed as a continuation of the McMath tradition to improve educational opportunity.

Nor was Faubus an instinctive racist. Coming from the hills as he did, his association with African Americans was minimal until World War II. He was more aligned with his father, Sam Faubus, socialist that he was, who viewed the blacks as other beleaguered workers in the fight against the capitalists during the 1930s.[7]

Under McMath's tutelage, Faubus became nimble, resourceful, and pragmatic. He watched, and he learned. And he did not harbor political grudges. If you were the powerful Little Rock attorney Bill Smith, who had worked with Francis Cherry to defeat

Faubus and now agreed to help him in the 1957 legislative session, Faubus would welcome you into the fold. Ditto for W. R. "Witt" Stephens, also a staunch Cherry supporter and owner of Arkansas Louisiana Gas Company. Stephens, a political master, was a Warwick in Arkansas politics and gravitated toward political power. It was Stephens's design to supplant Arkansas Power and Light Company as the dominant utility in the state with his gas company, and he was well on his way.[8]

In his first two legislative sessions as governor in 1955 and 1957, Faubus was viewed as a moderate and as a successful chief executive, especially in 1957. The legislature convened in January, and by its adjournment in March it had passed the Faubus Plan, which included a one-cent increase in the sales tax, a longer school year, teacher-pay increases, pay increases for judges and prosecutors, and an overhaul of the State Hospital for the mentally ill.[9]

But, as governor, he had also welcomed African Americans into the leadership of the Democratic Party, appointed blacks to state boards, integrated state colleges, and equalized pay for black state employees. There were whispers: Was Orval Faubus, in fact, a Communist? He was most certainly not acting like a southern good ole boy, and conservatives in the state, particularly conservatives on racial politics, began to look askance at him.[10]

The U.S. Supreme Court's 1954 decision in *Brown v. Board of Education,* which struck down state segregation laws for the public schools, also loomed large. There had been about five relatively quiet desegregations in public schools in Arkansas, including Charleston, which was Dale Bumpers's hometown. Then came Hoxie in 1955 and former state senator Jim Johnson. Hoxie was not quiet and drew exaggerated attention in the press, both statewide and nationally. The integrated white school with only twenty-one newly enrolled blacks was featured in *Life* magazine in an article titled "A Morally Right Decision."[11]

In the wake of that article, Jim Johnson and other white supremacists had rolled into Hoxie to thwart integration and had only been subdued by a federal court injunction. That had not stopped Johnson from painting Faubus as an integrationist who was undermining the "southern way of life." Johnson then ran against Faubus for governor in 1956 on the race issue. He was defeated overwhelmingly, but he wanted to run again. In August 1957, Faubus had been told by his pollster, Gene Newsom, that Johnson's support was growing.

Much later, Faubus would tell Johnson, "You made me take positions that served me well politically."[12] It was a frank and candid acknowledgment that Johnson had pushed Faubus to the right and eventually into the segregationist camp. But it really began in 1956 with his race against Johnson. Though Johnson lost the race for governor, he had won a race on a completely different front. He had proposed an initiated act by the people to memorialize states' rights in the Arkansas Constitution. On November 6, 1956, at the general election, the people of Arkansas adopted the act, which became Amendment 44 and which authorized the General Assembly to oppose the 1954 *Brown* decision, which, in effect, had desegregated the nation's public schools. Amendment 44 endorsed "interposing the sovereignty of the State of Arkansas to the end of nullification of these and all deliberate palpable and dangerous invasions of or encroachments upon the rights and powers not delegated to the United States."[13]

Then, during the 1957 legislative session, various anti-integration measures soared through the General Assembly, including one to establish a State Sovereignty Commission with investigative powers into suspect affiliations by Arkansans and to prevent federal interference with states' rights.[14] Another act provided that no child could be forced to attend integrated schools.[15] A third authorized funds for legal counsel to represent school boards fighting the *Brown* decision.[16] Jim Johnson's fine hand could be seen behind all these efforts, but Faubus was not recalcitrant in the face of the segregationist onslaught. Far from it. He signed each bill into law.

The legislative session, though, was not where Jim Johnson operated at his most nefarious. Again, in later years, he admitted to orchestrating a barrage of telephone calls to Faubus—"hustling him" as he put it—to convey the threat of violence.[17] Added to this was the fact that Jimmy Karam, a local haberdasher and hanger-on, had moved into the governor's mansion and was screening calls to allow only calls to Faubus from staunch segregationists who warned about the threat of violence. It was Karam who made overtures to the segregationist White Citizens Council on behalf of Faubus. According to the colloquy set out in Roy Reed's biography, *Faubus,* Karam called Amis Guthridge and asked whether his group would support Faubus if he stopped integration at Central High. Guthridge responded yes. "All right, he wants to meet with you," Karam is quoted as saying.[18]

The integration of Central High was only a few days away, and Faubus had begun to survey the landscape. He had been painted as a perfidious proponent of integration by Jim Johnson for his past actions as governor. He had seen his popularity vis-à-vis Jim Johnson wane in recent months, as evidenced by the Newsom polls. He had received reports about impending violence, but Superintendent Blossom would not openly admit that might be the case or ask for help. Faubus also knew that standing up against integration at Central High would catapult him into a third term as governor in 1958. His personal staff members in the governor's office, especially Jimmy Karam, were pushing him toward the segregationist position. He had not heard from old liberal friends like Sid McMath, Harry Ashmore, and Ed Dunaway, directly, that is, until the weekend before the schools were to open; nor had he reached out to them for advice.[19] More and more, as he weighed his various options, only one course of action began to emerge.

What crystallized the course for him was a state court lawsuit brought by a member of the Central High Mothers League to delay forced integration of Central High School.[20] At the ensuing hearing on the petition, Blossom's board did not support delay, and Blossom testified he had no reason to believe violence would occur. Faubus was surprised at Blossom's testimony; but in his own testimony, he advised the judge that an unusual number of guns had been sold in gun shops in central Arkansas and caravans of armed men were preparing to descend on Little Rock. The chancery judge, Murray Reed, ordered the integration to come to a halt that same day, August 29, 1957. On August 30, an imported federal district judge, Ronald N. Davis from North Dakota, disagreed and ordered Central High to be integrated the first day of school, which was September 3.[21]

Later during the FBI investigation of what violence was really imminent, the Blossom forces and the Faubus people called each other "liars."[22] Accusations and recriminations flew fast and furiously back and forth about who knew what about potential violence. Blossom said he only called on Faubus to make a plea for peaceful integration. Bill Smith, Faubus's lawyer, countered that Blossom was adamant that Faubus had to act to stop integration. Of course, Jim Johnson's minions had imparted information about violence to both men. Johnson was their Svengali.

It was early in the morning, Labor Day, September 2, and Faubus had made his decision. He would mobilize the National Guard to surround Central High School and prevent the African American students from entering the next day, which was the first day of school. Even his faithful counselor Bill Smith, he knew, would initially balk at the idea. And his economic development director, Winthrop Rockefeller, would tell him that calling out the Guard would be a blow to the state and to industrial development. And Virgil Blossom? Blossom had vacillated on the threat of violence and the need for protection of the students and public officials. The Little Rock School Board members were a bunch of integrationists, he mused. Harry Ashmore and the *Arkansas Gazette* would not like it either, but they were out of touch with the Arkansas people.

Faubus knew he was right. The Guard would prevent even the possibility of a race riot, and integration would be stalled. He would also preempt Jim Johnson and his pride of rabid segregationists on the race issue and seize it as his own. It was a brilliant political strategy.

And that is what he did. The Guard was mobilized to surround Central High on September 2 at 9:00 p.m. At 10:15 p.m., Faubus appeared on television to explain his decision. He began by underscoring the violence that would occur from integration and the fact that both races were arming. He said litigation over the segregation laws was ongoing and should be given a chance to play out. He said his objective was peace. He concluded by saying the Guard could not keep the peace "if forcible integration is carried out tomorrow in the schools of this community." Hence, he said "the inevitable conclusion" was that the schools "must be operated on the same basis as they have been operated in the past."

The Rubicon had been crossed. Governor Faubus had just proclaimed that he would use the Guard to keep Central High segregated.

Orval Faubus announces that he is deploying the Arkansas National Guard, September 2, 1957. *Published with permission of the* Arkansas Democrat-Gazette, *copyright September 3, 1957.*

Faubus's motives for calling out the National Guard to prevent integration at Central High remains a subject of fierce debate even to this day. But there is no real debate over the *effect* of his decision. It transformed what was largely a local issue over school desegregation in one community into a state issue. And with the federal district court response by Judge Ronald Davies to remove the National Guard, and, ultimately, the deployment of the 101st

Airborne Division into Little Rock by President Dwight D. Eisenhower, the state issue became the most significant constitutional crisis the country had faced since the Civil War.

Before his recent death, Jim Johnson described the Orval Faubus of 1957 as one who watched where people were heading and then "before long he would ease up beside them and then move out in front and say he was leading them all the time." What got Faubus, Johnson recalled, was the overwhelming success of the Interposition Amendment for states' rights in 1956 (Amendment 44).[23] Johnson was the key force in having the initiated act that led to the amendment placed on the ballot and passed, and he kept the names of the canvassers and signers for the amendment. Those names would later become his core group of supporters, and he would use that list in his campaigns against Winthrop Rockefeller for governor and J. William Fulbright for the U.S. Senate and to aid Senator John McClellan in his race against David Pryor.

Faubus, Johnson said, never had an "emotional issue against blacks. There were no blacks in Madison County. It wasn't personal with him. He just wanted to be governor for life."[24] When questioned as to whether he had any "heads-up" that Faubus would call out the National Guard to stop integration, Johnson said Faubus had sent word to Johnson to have his friends at Central High the morning of September 3 because he was "going to do something that might please [Johnson] very much."[25] When Johnson heard Faubus had surrounded Central High with the National Guard, he was "dumbfounded." This was "totally out of the blue," he added. "How can you be more dramatic than that?" he asked rhetorically.[26]

Johnson, though he is credited with orchestrating a campaign to make Faubus believe violence was imminent at Central High, said recently, "Faubus knew there was no prospect of violence. That was his excuse, which our group supplied him."[27] "There was less violence at Central High," he added, "than on the sideline of a usual high school football game."[28] His group, Johnson said, was largely docile and believed in the cause. The Little Rock Police Department could easily have handled the situation.

Johnson found, he said, that Faubus was "a fast learner" and became a leader among old South recalcitrants like Senator Jim Eastland of Mississippi and Senator Richard Russell of Georgia.[29] After the "invasion," as he termed it, by the federal troops on September 24, 1957, the mission was to keep Faubus "in line" and make sure he did not "cave in" to more moderate forces.[30]

But, in addition to Johnson's view, Faubus's position that he called out the National Guard only to thwart violence does not stand the test of time or meaningful scrutiny. To be sure, there had been hecklers at Central High on September 4, 1957, the taunting of Little Rock Nine member Elizabeth Eckford being the most famous pictorial example. And there were toughs who beat African American reporters and fist fights that broke out around Central High after the National Guard was removed on Monday, September 23. This precipitated the federal military action, which was the deployment of the 101st Airborne Division the following day.

However, before he called out the National Guard, Faubus told Winthrop Rockefeller that were he to enforce the federal court order to desegregate with state forces, "soon after the next election you [Rockefeller] would be working for Jim Johnson."[31] It was a clear reference to the political threat he perceived from his racist adversary.

It also begs the question of why Faubus could not have used the National Guard to control any potential violence *and* protect the entry of the Little Rock Nine into Central High on September 4. Clearly, he could have. He may have believed violence of some degree was imminent through the machinations of Jim Johnson and the telephone campaign. He soon learned, though, that there was a paucity of FBI intelligence to that effect.

The simple answer was that Faubus would not enforce the federal desegregation of Central High, occasioned by the *Brown* decision, with state troops. It was the job of the federal government. He said as much in his autobiography *Down from the Hills*.[32] He was equally astounded that the federal government had no mechanism in place to enforce the *Brown* decisions.

What about his duty to enforce the State Constitution with Amendment 44 and the legislation he had signed into law during the 1957 legislative session? There is the argument that Faubus had no choice but to enforce the laws of his state and his state constitution. Still and again, Faubus was adroit enough to know that federal law, including Supreme Court decisions, were the supreme law of the land under the U.S. Constitution.

So Faubus made a Faustian decision to block integration at Central High in 1957. His advisors and Jim Johnson's unabashed engagement in fear-mongering were instrumental in that decision. Faubus would subsequently tell David Pryor he thought they would have agreed on most issues "if it hadn't been for the people around us."[33] For certain, Faubus did not listen to Winthrop Rockefeller, Little Rock grande dame Adolphine Terry, and others who tried to dissuade him from his course of conduct. Nor did he call for advice from old friends like Sid McMath, Ed Dunaway, and Henry Woods. He was off on a ride that would cement his place at the seat of power in the state for ten more years. And in the process he became the face of Arkansas. As Harry Ashmore later wrote, "I never questioned Faubus's assertion that he was not a

Orval Faubus as the consummate politician on the campaign trail.
Published with permission of the Arkansas Democrat-Gazette, *copyright December 15, 1994.*

racist; it was unabashed expediency, and not conviction, that determined his course."[34]

The years since 1957 have placed Orval Faubus firmly on the wrong side of history. It must have pained him to see his personal political currency become virtually worthless in his later years. He made his choice, and it benefited him, but only in the short term. His legacy is forever tarnished by a decision that was so totally wrong. The blemish he left in Arkansas, the South, and, indeed, the whole country in the eyes of the world has yet to be completely removed. Granted, it would have taken a supreme act of courage on his part to facilitate the desegregation of Central High School. It might even have cost him his devoutly-to-be-wished third term as governor. But he did nothing to ease the situation or to appeal to the best instincts of the people of this state. That would fall to later governors—Rockefeller, Bumpers, Pryor, Clinton, and Tucker—who spent much of their terms striving to resurrect the state and to remove the stain that Faubus had caused.

Winthrop Rockefeller
1967–1971

For unto whomsoever much is given, of him shall be much required.

—LUKE 12:48, KING JAMES BIBLE

Winthrop Rockefeller lifted his hulking six-foot four-inch frame from his chair and lumbered across his study at the governor's mansion. His wife, Jeannette, sat still and watched him evenly. The day before, Thursday, April 4, 1968, Dr. Martin Luther King Jr. had been shot and killed on the balcony of the Lorraine Motel in Memphis, Tennessee. Rockefeller had publicly dubbed the act "deplorable."[1] The question now was what else needed to be done to quell the gathering storm. Riots had already broken out in Washington, D.C.; Chicago; Baltimore; and across the country. Arkansas would not be spared the incidents of gunfire and arson the following day, particularly in the cities of Pine Bluff, Hot Springs, and North Little Rock.[2]

The Rockefellers were united on one score. A day of mourning for the coming Sunday needed to be announced by executive proclamation. It had been Jeannette's idea. The proclamation had already been drafted, and, in addition to the day of mourning, the proclamation espoused calm and the eradication of

Winthrop Rockefeller as governor. *Courtesy of Butler Center photos, Arkansas Studies Institute Collection, Little Rock.*

racial barriers and prayed for a joining together "to fulfill the vision of brotherhood that gave purpose to Martin Luther King's life and works."[3]

Simultaneous with the proclamation, black leaders led by Dr. Jerry Jewell, president of the state NAACP, were coordinating a memorial service on the state capitol steps for Sunday afternoon, April 7. Secretary of State Kelly Bryant had agreed to the service, but Rockefeller had not yet committed to an appearance. He had expressed a desire to speak at a later interdenominational memorial service at the request of Episcopal Bishop Robert R. Brown, to be held at Trinity Episcopal Cathedral in Little Rock.[4]

There were now two issues for the governor and Jeannette to resolve. The first was what Rockefeller would say to his department heads in a meeting in just a few hours about the assassination this Friday morning. The second was whether Rockefeller would, in fact, attend the service on the capitol steps on Sunday. His security force had already emphatically told him that if he did attend, he would be fair game for any sniper, black or white, positioned in any building across from the capitol. Plus, there were the obvious political consequences of supporting Dr. King even in death. Rockefeller had a ready excuse for not attending the memorial service—a binding commitment to speak in Hot Springs at one thirty that afternoon had long been on his calendar. The governor looked at Jeannette and spoke evenly: "We have to honor King's legacy, and I'm going to tell my department heads precisely that."

What he did say later that morning to eighty-five assembled state officials was that they needed to be more aggressive in finding job opportunities for blacks in state government to eliminate "the cause" of Dr. King's tragic death. He added, bobbing his head back and forth: "The problem is no different today than it was yesterday. The tragedy, I think, focuses a new attention on it. But I think we ought to intensify our efforts and search our consciences to see whether we are doing our part."[5]

Friday night and Saturday, fires and shootings spread across the state. In Pine Bluff, seven hundred National Guardsmen patrolled the streets after four firebomb attacks and a gun fight that wounded three men. Hot Springs reported four fires. In North Little Rock, there was gunfire and a black-on-white beating.[6] Racial tension was palpable, and the state hunkered down for what was believed to be the worst yet to come.

He had moved to Arkansas in 1953 to divorce his first wife, Bobo Sears, and at the request of Arkansas army friend, Frank Newell.[7] Before then, Rockefeller had been the stuff of tabloids. "Playboy" and "rebel" were his common monikers. He was a grandson of the great oil titan and robber baron, John D. Rockefeller, and was born to extraordinary wealth and privilege. But he had always eschewed the Rockefeller trappings and any sense of seriousness and commitment, with the exception of a distinguished military career in World War II, where he was awarded the Bronze Star with clusters. Wife Bobo, for example, had been a "dance hall" girl.

Rockefeller, though, was more than his public persona, and Arkansas provided the perfect stage where he could prove that to the world, and to his family. It could not have been more different than New York. He needed the proper venue for his creation, and he found that atop Petit Jean Mountain outside of Morrilton, where he purchased 927 acres and began the arduous task of clearing and irrigating his land. He invested in Santa Gertrudis cattle and a grass farm. He took on a rancher's dress, replete with Stetson hat and cowboy boots. His rancher image suited him. Arkansas quickly became his adopted home.

But he needed a partner, and he found one in Jeannette Edris from Seattle. They married in 1956 and proved an indomitable team. If anything, she was more fervent about black equality. If Winthrop was almost color blind concerning race, and he was, Jeannette was convinced that African Americans had been held back by economic circumstances and inequitable educational opportunity—not by racial inferiority.

In truth, Rockefeller did not know from whence his sense of equality had sprung. He certainly hailed from the North and was raised in privileged circumstances few could appreciate. With wealth came an ingrained commitment to give back to others, perhaps spawned by his Baptist faith and by an insecurity associated with the guilt of the Rockefeller fortune. He believed he had always been that way. His friendship with servants, service in the armed forces, and roustabouting in the oil fields of Texas all led to close associations with those who worked with their hands and with African Americans in particular.

Plus, he had always had a real empathy for the underdog, perhaps because of his perceived status as such in the eyes of his family. No people fell as readily into this category as did the African Americans. In Texas, he had seen his African American maid denied health care in white hospitals and black veterans denied equal jobs and equal pay.[8] It appalled him. Quietly and methodically, he began using his money to foment change. He desegregated all public accommodations in Colonial Williamsburg in Virginia when he took over as foundation chair in 1953.[9] When he spread his largesse to the Morrilton public schools, he required desegregation as a precondition to receiving the money.[10] As a zealous supporter of the Urban League, in the Rockefeller family tradition, he bemoaned the snail's pace at which desegregation was taking place.[11]

After he moved to Arkansas, he found himself to be a stranger in a strange land. Still, he knew intuitively, this was where he could and would make his mark. For he saw the great potential in Arkansas and also saw what was holding it back: ineffective political leadership; a lingering hillbilly image fostered by such iconoclasts as *Baltimore Sun* editorialist H. L. Mencken; the crippling blow from the Central High School crisis in 1957, which painted Little Rock and, indeed, the whole state as backward and racist; and the failures in public education and business development. He knew he could effect change by his commitment, by his connections, and by force of will.

He first became head of Governor Faubus's Arkansas Industrial Development Commission in 1955.[12] The Rockefeller name was electric and out-of-state businesses, still skittish about an Arkansas home, took notice. But then came the stigma of 1957, and he was convinced that Orval Faubus personified that stigma. He resolved to do something about it, and he ran for governor against Faubus in 1964 as a Republican. He lost in a respectable race, winning 43 percent of the vote.[13] He quickly pledged to run again in 1966, and this time Faubus removed himself as an opponent. Rockefeller defeated the Democratic nominee, former Supreme Court justice and avowed segregationist Jim Johnson, in a brutal campaign where Johnson called him a "prissy sissy" and "Madison Avenue Cowboy."[14] Rockefeller won 54.4 percent of the vote.[15] *Time Magazine* placed Rockefeller on its cover in a December 2, 1966, issue. He had earned the spurs to go with the boots.

His campaign in the Mississippi Delta region was largely the reason for his victory. The Delta covers much of eastern Arkansas with its heavily black population, and African Americans had left the Democratic Party and supported Rockefeller by a margin of three to one.[16] Part of the reason was the ideological backlash against Jim Johnson's trademark racism and his refusal to shake

Winthrop Rockefeller in his rancher persona on Petit Jean Mountain. *Courtesy of Butler Center photos, Arkansas Studies Institute Collection, Little Rock.*

hands with African American groups on the campaign trail.[17] Part was due to superb organizational efforts fueled by Rockefeller money, which used the black church network and get-out-the-vote efforts with transportation to the polls.

In office, WR, as he was called, kept his pledge to promote African Americans in state government. William "Sonny" Walker was appointed the first black department head in state government, as director of the Office of Economic Opportunity.[18] He also appointed NAACP Legal Defense Fund attorney John Walker to the State Education Board, but the Arkansas Senate balked at the nomination and refused to confirm it overwhelmingly. Rockefeller next appointed another African American, Dr. William Townsend, who met a similar fate in the Senate. He subsequently settled on Episcopal priest Emery Washington, another African American, who was confirmed.

He commissioned a study on enhancing racial opportunity in Arkansas. When the General Assembly refused to authorize a state Human Resources Council, Rockefeller set up one of his own by executive order, half black and half white, and appointed an African American, Ozell Sutton, as its executive director. He appointed blacks in various positions throughout the state. At the end of his second term as governor, he would commute the death sentences of everyone on death row, fifteen men, eleven of whom were African American.[19] Six of the African Americans were on death row for rape, which was later removed from the list of capital offenses where the death penalty could be imposed.[20]

The memorial service on the capitol steps organized by NAACP president Jerry Jewell and Reverend Cecil Cone, pastor of the Union African Methodist Episcopal (AME) Church, began with "God Bless America" and "America the Beautiful," followed by Negro spirituals. Prominent clergy spoke, including Bishop

Robert R. Brown of the Episcopal Church, Bishop Albert L. Fletcher of the Roman Catholic Diocese of Little Rock, Bishop Paul V. Galloway of the Methodist Church, Rabbi E. E. Palnick of Temple B'nai Israel, and Reverend W. O. Vaught of Immanuel Baptist Church. Following those remarks, the tenor of the service changed. Dr. Jewell railed against discrimination against blacks in housing, jobs, and education and concluded with a not-so-veiled threat: "The youth of today no longer will accept the old order. . . . In a riot we all lose but they say Negroes have nothing to lose. You figure that one out."[21] Reverend Cone followed with a threat of his own and implored Governor Rockefeller to act: "Our governor must take the lead. Our two mayors must take the lead. The power structure downtown must take the lead or there will be no downtown."[22]

The crowd meanwhile had swelled from one thousand to three thousand, two-thirds of whom were black. There was applause for Reverend Cone as Rockefeller strode out of the capitol and took a seat next to the lectern and microphone. He had just arrived from Hot Springs, and his staff and the police repeated their warnings against attending the service because of the obvious danger and political consequences.[23] But he and Jeannette disagreed. It was a day for healing, and their public and profoundly expressed grief was a vital symbol and tonic for the time. They also knew Arkansas was the only state to hold such a public service and that their participation would be valuable oil poured upon the troubled waters.

Rockefeller was the final speaker. He was not a gifted public speaker, but he stood erect behind the lectern, clutching it with both hands, and voiced his optimism that Arkansas now, unlike in 1957, was on the threshold of leading the nation in human relations. "Let us not forget the importance of equal education," he added. "Let us not forget the importance of environment. Let

Winthrop Rockefeller at Martin Luther King memorial service on the state capitol steps, April 7, 1968. *University of Arkansas at Little Rock Library Collection.*

us not forget the elimination of the slums and ghettos. Let us not forget that we are all creatures of God."[24] When he finished, he clasped the hands of two black leaders, and with Jeannette they boldly sang "We Shall Overcome." But the Reverend Cecil Cone was still emotional.

Biographer John Ward writes that Rockefeller later told him: "When Cecil Cone began to agitate the crowd after the meeting was over and just before the benediction, I just stepped forward and put my hand on his shoulder and in a very firm tone I said, 'I think now is the time for the benediction.'"[25] Against the provocative Reverend Cone, Rockefeller was a placating force.

Rockefeller's sincerity and heartfelt sorrow won the hearts and minds of those present, and he was mobbed by an affectionate crowd when the service ended. This was April 7, 1968. In seven months, he would meet the Democratic Party nominee for governor, Marion Crank, in the general election. He defeated Crank in a close race, winning only 51 percent of the vote. Many reasons have been offered for the slimness of the victory, and one, no doubt, was the reaction of some whites to his role in the memorial service for Dr. King. Conservative pundits speculated at the time that Rockefeller's participation in the service was a political misstep.

The legacy of Winthrop Rockefeller is rich and varied, and it pervades the Arkansas fabric. It includes his attacks on the corruption of the past whether it was illegal gambling in Hot Springs, the anemic regulation of the insurance and securities industries, or the inhumane trusty system in our state prisons. His vision, though, was always for the future. He proposed numerous reforms in such disparate fields as taxation, education, and efficiency in state government. For many reforms, it fell to Dale Bumpers, his successor, to actually shepherd the legislation through the General Assembly. But Rockefeller was the catalyst. It was he who planted the seeds that ultimately came to fruition.

One biographer describes Rockefeller as a racial moderate, but regardless of the label, former legal aide and now federal district judge G. Thomas Eisele believes he represented the turning point in race relations in Arkansas.[26] That was not his purpose, Eisele adds, but it was "part of his overall philosophy."[27]

Today, his former close aides agree that Rockefeller never "backed away" from racial conflict.[28] And, no doubt, his greatest success was his tireless work on behalf of minorities in Arkansas, illustrated best by this simple, symbolic gesture on April 7, 1968, on the state capitol steps. Those who knew Winthrop Rockefeller were not surprised. His dignity, leadership, and grace in the face of considerable danger, political and otherwise, served to diffuse an explosive situation. He set an example of how best to act in time of crisis and to be guided by what is in our hearts.

Dale Bumpers as governor. *Arkansas History Commission Collection.*

Dale Bumpers
1971–1975

I've always believed that politics is an honorable calling.

—WILL BUMPERS

The room slowly filled on the first floor of the state capitol for the seven o'clock meeting held each morning during the 1973 legislative session.[1] Staff, legislative floor managers, and department heads attended. When the governor walked in, everyone stood, then sat, and Dale Bumpers began talking about what was uppermost in his mind—a Senate bill introduced by Senator Guy "Mutt" Jones of Faulkner County to split the Fifth Judicial District for blatantly political reasons. The district was made up of five counties, and the split was orchestrated by its legislative sponsors so that two of those counties (Faulkner and Conway) could become the political fiefdom of circuit judge Russell Roberts and state senator Guy "Mutt" Jones of Faulkner County and Sheriff Marlin Hawkins of Conway County. This political triumvirate was infamous in the state for its political clout, and their suspect political practices are best illustrated by Sheriff Hawkins's autobiography, *How I Stole Elections*.[2] Their ploy would leave Alex Streett, the young reform prosecutor who had been a political thorn in their flesh as he investigated corrupt election practices, isolated in what remained of the Fifth Judicial District. It was a dastardly plot to solidify power in Roberts, Jones, and Hawkins, and Bumpers recognized it for what it was.

At one point during the morning discussion, a brazen staffer blurted out that public officials and lawyers in Faulkner and Conway counties should be ashamed of themselves for not opposing this obvious political maneuver. Then he expanded his charge and tarred all the people of both counties with the brush of corruption. Smiling, Bumpers's gifted legislative aide, Richard Arnold, spoke up and echoed Abraham's plea to God on behalf of Sodom and Gomorrah: "If there are only ten righteous people in those counties, will you save them?" For the moment, there was laughter and the tension was broken

Representative Tom Sparks of Fordyce, who was a House floor leader for Bumpers, stood next, and the room fell silent. He said, "This is the greatest moral issue you will face this legislative session." Everyone in the room nodded their heads in agreement.

Several weeks later, Dale Bumpers looked out the window of the governor's office to the north, as the afternoon sun began to dip, and the April shadows to fall. Across from him sat his legislative aide, Richard Arnold, who briefed him on enacted legislation for him to sign, or veto. Neither man had spoken for thirty minutes.[3] The bill, Senate Bill 283, that lay before him was Senator Jones's bill to divide the Fifth Judicial District. It had easily passed both houses of the General Assembly. No other bill during the1973 legislative session had caused Bumpers such consternation as this piece of legislation. In fact, the session had been successful for Bumpers by anyone's standards. Legislation he had touted included free textbooks for public high schools, publicly funded kindergarten for public education, and a $30 million appropriation for the University Medical School System. All of it had passed.

Yet, vetoing the bill that lay before him could sound the death knell for his quest for a third term as governor or a term in the U.S. Senate due to the political antagonism a veto would engender. To sign the bill, on the other hand, would be an endorsement of political corruption, and Bumpers knew it. That said, he had been urged to sign the bill by many of the politically astute in the state, including no less a personage than Congressman Wilbur Mills, the esteemed chairman of the House Ways and Means Committee, who was at the peak of his political power and had not yet fallen from grace due to his escapade with the stripper Fanne Foxe. Mills had made the telephone call to Bumpers, according to Sheriff Marlin Hawkins, in Hawkins's presence.[4]

If the truth be known, this was the sort of moment for which Bumpers had always been prepared. Raised as a forward-thinking Methodist who believed, as he often said, that when he got to heaven, F.D.R. would greet him at the pearly gates, Bumpers also believed politics and public service were noble callings. His father, Will Bumpers, who had served in the General Assembly, had instilled that orthodoxy in his son in the small mountain hamlet of Charleston, where he operated the town hardware store and had nightly political discussions around the dining room table with Bumpers and his two siblings—Carroll, who was the older brother, and Maggie, who was indomitable in every way. Bumpers learned the talent of consummate story telling around the table and in his father's hardware store as he listened to the men spin their yarns. And he also developed a wicked sense of humor. This would soon enhance his rhetorical skills as a trial lawyer, Sunday school teacher, and stump speaker. His humor, in particular, was highly effective in relaxing and engaging his audience before he slipped in a more serious message.

Tragically, both of Bumpers's parents would be killed in a car accident by a drunk driver in 1949. Before their deaths, Lattie and Will Bumpers had openly cried as eighteen-year-old Dale climbed onto the bus at Charleston during the early morning hours for his marine training and long trek to Japan to begin the final invasion.[5] The year was 1943. As he was en route to Japan in 1945, the bombing of Hiroshima and Nagasaki occurred and then Japan's unconditional surrender. He returned home, attended the University of Arkansas at Fayetteville, and earned a law degree from Northwestern University. Ultimately, he returned to Charleston to practice law and operate the family hardware store. He married Betty Flannigan, and they had three children.

But his father's message on politics gnawed at him, and he often harkened back to his trip to Booneville with his father and Carroll to see President Franklin Roosevelt when he was only ten.[6] The boys knew how much Will revered Roosevelt, and Dale was prepared to see perfection incarnate.

"Look at that man," Will Bumpers said to his sons. "That's the president of the United States." Franklin Roosevelt was being helped to the back of the train car by his son, James. It was obvious he could not walk. Dale and Carroll stared hard at the president. "What's wrong with him?" Dale finally ventured. "I'll tell you later," his father said.

And on the drive from Booneville to Charleston, he did. "The president had polio," Will said. "He got it when he was in his thirties. He can't walk." The boys digested this for a moment. Their hero had a defect. It was difficult for Dale to comprehend a Franklin Roosevelt who was not grand in every way.

Will Bumpers went on, his eyes fixed on the two-lane county

road: "If Franklin Roosevelt with polio, unable to walk, can become president of the United States, just think what you two boys can be. You got your bodies; you got good minds. There's no reason you can't be president, too."

It was clear to young Dale that his father meant it and that he had just been anointed a presidential contender.

Once he entered politics, no one was better on the hustings than Dale Bumpers. Bill Clinton, early on, recognized the Bumpers gift and "went to school" on Bumpers's speaking style. Clinton's respect for Bumpers's oratory became abundantly clear when he chose his mentor to give the closing argument at his impeachment trial before the U.S. Senate in 1998. Bumpers's talk was poignant, witty, practical, and steeped in common sense.[7] One *New York Times* columnist compared it to Pericles's funeral oration.[8] High praise indeed.

But that was twenty-five years later. Now Bumpers wrestled in his office with his moral dilemma. He knew that there probably was a need for an additional judge in the current Fifth Judicial District due to a heavy caseload. But he also knew the manifest reason for splitting off two counties (Faulkner and Conway) to form the Twentieth Judicial District was to rid Sheriff Hawkins, Senator Mutt Jones, and Judge Roberts of a major irritant, prosecuting attorney Alex Streett.

The turmoil within that judicial district had reached a boiling point after Streett was elected its prosecuting attorney. He had called a grand jury to investigate election fraud, particularly evident in a state Senate race, as well as suspect jury verdicts in Conway County.[9] Judge Roberts had convened his own special grand jury to tell election officials to ignore Streett's investigation. Both Roberts and Streett sought to put the other in jail.[10] Shouting matches were known to occur in Roberts's chambers between the two men.

None of the three principals in the Fifth Judicial District ploy—Hawkins, Jones, and Roberts—had been friends or supporters of Dale Bumpers. Indeed, they were part of the old Democratic Party machine, together with Representative Paul Van Dalsem of Perry County, that Faubus had institutionalized and that Bumpers, and Rockefeller before him, had fought so hard to dismantle. That would make vetoing the bill all the easier for Bumpers, especially since Bumpers had defeated Faubus in the run off for governor three years earlier.

Dale Bumpers, nonetheless, was an ambitious man and had no intention of going back to Charleston after two terms as governor. A third term beckoned to him or, more to his liking, a race that his political consultant, Deloss Walker, championed against J. William Fulbright for the U.S. Senate. Though each person in the room the morning of Tom Sparks's speech agreed with the representative about the moral issue, few doubted that a veto of the Fifth Judicial District bill would cost Bumpers dearly. Bumpers had already lost one political race that few in Arkansas knew about—a race for state representative in 1962 from his home county, Franklin County.[11] A second loss, he knew, would damage his career, perhaps irrevocably. In that case, Will Bumpers's admonition about the presidency would be all for naught.

And there was something else. Bumpers had vetoed one politically sensitive bill during this session, Senate Bill 106, which mandated that city and county governments receive each year a fixed 7 percent of annual revenues. In Bumpers's mind, this would hamstring the legislature in appropriating funds. The Municipal League and Association of County Judges had lobbied hard for the legislation and had gotten it passed. After Bumpers exercised his veto on February 6, 1973, he emphasized in his veto message the limiting effect a fixed percentage of revenues dedicated to the cities and counties would have on legislative flexibility.[12] A motion was made to override that veto, and the motion failed. Yet, the vote had been extremely close.

Bumpers was often depicted in the media as a young Lochinvar on a white steed who had ridden in from the west to vanquish the corrupt old guard associated primarily with Orval Faubus and W. R. "Witt" Stephens of Arkansas Louisiana Gas Company. Faubus had been governor for twelve years and his appointments and friends in the General Assembly were entrenched. It was not so much a loyalty to Faubus that still abided in the legislature. After all, he had abandoned the office when he decided not to run against Rockefeller in 1966 and had been soundly defeated by Bumpers in 1970. It was more the accepted old way of doing business which involved exchanges of political favors and sweetheart deals. Bumpers threatened all of that.

Rockefeller without question had been a true breath of fresh air in Arkansas governance, but Rockefeller was largely ineffective in working with the General Assembly to pass his programs. It fell to Bumpers to implement many of Rockefeller's ideas, including raising the state income tax and reorganizing state departments and agencies. Therein lay the problem with many of the old hands in the General Assembly and especially in the Senate. If they could challenge a Bumpers veto successfully, Bumpers's effectiveness as governor would be eviscerated.

Bumpers knew this, and it weighed heavily on him. More than the 7 percent issue, the Fifth Judicial District bill pitted the old guard and political corruption against a leader who represented the new South and a new way of doing business. However, if Bumpers challenged the entrenched interests in the legislature and lost, his future as governor would be severely compromised.[13] Should he risk it?

George Fisher exhibits Dale Bumpers's prowess with the General Assembly. *Published with permission of the* Arkansas Democrat-Gazette, *copyright February 22, 1972. Arkansas Arts Center Library Collection of George Fisher Cartoons.*

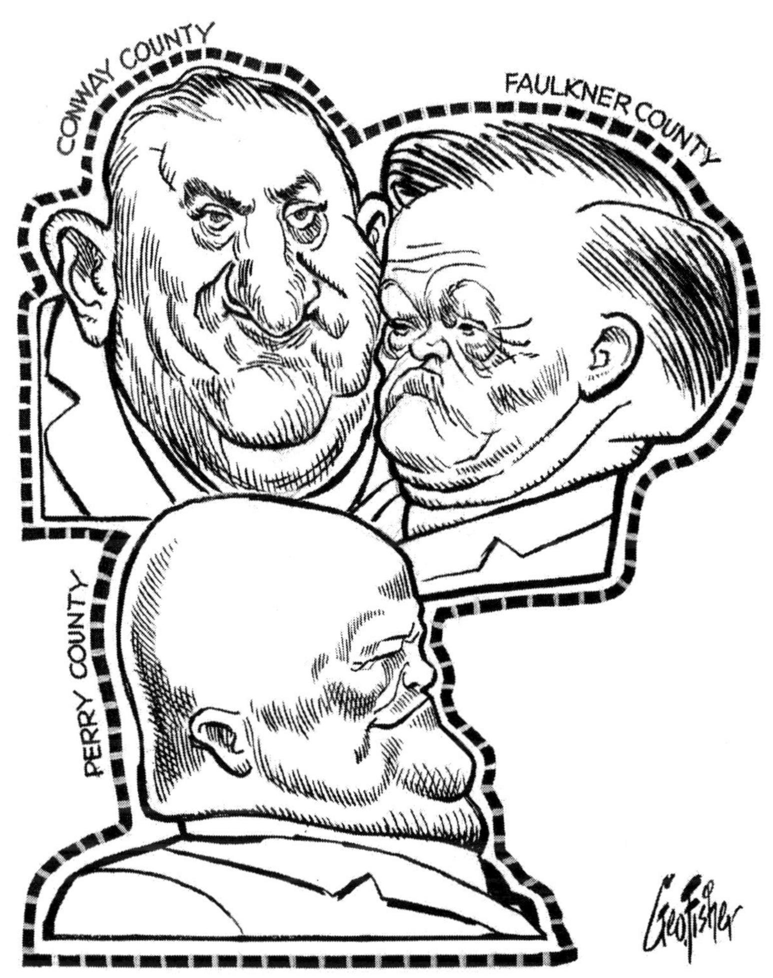

Shape Of The Proposed New Judicial District.

George Fisher lampoons the makeup of the new judicial district which ultimately did not include Perry County. *Published with permission of the* Arkansas Democrat-Gazette, *copyright December 24, 1972. Arkansas Arts Center Library Collection of George Fisher Cartoons.*

These and other thoughts raced through Dale Bumpers's mind as he sat with Richard Arnold in silence in the dimming afternoon light. Arnold, deferential to a fault, was not about to tell Bumpers what he should do. Bumpers, however, sensed how Arnold felt about the bill. Political fallout, though, was not for Arnold to weigh. That rested solely with Dale Bumpers.

Bumpers looked at his aide in the twilight: "What do you think, Richard?" Richard Arnold, who would eventually become chief judge of the U.S. Eighth Circuit Court of Appeals, did not answer. Arnold was not one to demonize people. Indeed, he saw good in most people.

"I think I should veto it," Bumpers finally said. And he did on March 5, 1973.[14]

Bumpers's veto message to the General Assembly was short and to the point. It stressed the high cost of creating a new judicial district with a new prosecuting attorney and additional staff. But the underlying message was there. Dale Bumpers would not sanction the old way of doing business and political corruption.

The battle, though, was not over. The General Assembly could still override Bumpers's veto by a simple majority vote. Unbeknownst to the bill's sponsors, two of Bumpers's floor leaders, Joe Woodward in the House and Martin Borchert in the Senate, had assiduously worked their respective chambers, even before the veto, to get commitments from the legislators not to override the veto if that contingency should occur. On March 6, 1973, the Senate voted to override the Bumpers veto.[15] A majority vote in the House was now needed for an effective override.

Ten days later the issue of the veto override went to the House of Representatives. Speaking against it was Representative Tom Sparks, who again couched the issue in terms of "the old politics against the new politics." "The case of the Fifth Judicial

District is a case of a bad judge," Sparks said, "kept in there by a bunch of lawyers who can profit from a bad situation." He added that the people of the Fifth District had elected a good prosecuting attorney. Those on the other side were frightened they would lose power, so they "made a grasp for power" with Senate Bill 283, Sparks said. He said Chief Justice Carleton Harris of the Arkansas Supreme Court could at any time assign special judges to the Fifth Judicial District to clean out the docket, if that was the problem. "You are about to do something which you may regret for the rest of this session, and possibly the rest of your life," Sparks said. He said that if the House overrode the veto of Senate Bill 283, the result would be chaos and "you'll have no leadership at all. . . . You have a good man of the new politics," Sparks said, and he said that some legislators were talking about going back to the old politics. "The people don't want it that way," he said.[16]

A vote was then taken, and the veto override failed in the House by four votes.[17]

Whatever fears Bumpers had about his political demise because of the veto soon proved to be unfounded. He began "campaigning" immediately after the session ended in April 1973 by giving a multitude of civic club speeches and holding regional meetings with his political coordinators. No one knew at that point what he would do. They just knew that he was running for something. Far from being his undoing, his stand against political corruption won praise around the state and became a decided political asset.

Bumpers ultimately chose to run for the Senate against Fulbright, an incumbent senator for twenty-four years and chairman of the Senate Foreign Relations Committee. It was a choice labeled by many progressive Democrats as fratricidal. It was

Dale Bumpers with author, 1973. *Author's files.*

Fulbright, ironically, who ultimately garnered the support of much of the Democratic Party establishment, whom Bumpers had angered with his Fifth Judicial District veto and by not doing political favors. Fulbright also had alienated many in Arkansas by his opposition to the Vietnam War, his perceived pro-Arab stance, his signing of the Southern Manifesto against desegregation in 1956, and his aloofness from his native state. Quoting from Willie Loman in Arthur Miller's play, "Death of a Salesman," Fulbright termed Bumpers a salesman "riding on a smile and a shoeshine." That was not enough to offset the Bumpers juggernaut; nor was it enough to salvage the race for Fulbright.

Dale Bumpers won the U.S. Senate seat by almost a two-to-one vote: 65 percent to 35 percent. It quickly catapulted him to the ranks of those talked about as presidential contenders in 1976. He was the giant killer now, who in four short years had dispatched three Arkansas icons—Orval Faubus, Winthrop Rockefeller, and J. William Fulbright. Perhaps Will Bumpers's dream was within reach for his son. But the laurels in 1976 went to Jimmy Carter. Bumpers later recognized that, though he flirted with a presidential race in years to come, 1976 had been the year for him.

Bumpers never shrank from telling people what he had done with the Fifth Judicial District veto. What that veto unquestionably did, though, was reinforce for Bumpers Truman's sage advice about the wisdom of the voting public.

Bumpers had visited the former president in Springfield, Missouri, in 1971 and had been whining about how difficult it was to make the decisions the governor of Arkansas was called upon to make.[18] Suddenly, it dawned on him that he was in the presence of the man who had made the decision to drop the atom bomb on Hiroshima and Nagasaki in order to win the war against Japan in 1945. Bumpers was suddenly chastened. He "hadn't liked President Truman," he later said, "until he fired General Douglas McArthur" for insubordination during the Korean War.[19] "I admired him so much for that," Bumpers maintained.

Truman had listened politely to Bumpers in his parlor, but now it was his turn to speak. He advised Bumpers to get the best advice possible before making a decision and then make it. More importantly, be honest with the people. "People can handle the truth," he said.[20] It was a compass that guided Bumpers throughout his political life.

Bumpers would later describe the Fifth Judicial District veto as one of the most difficult decisions he had to make as governor, if not the most difficult.[21] It could have been "lethal" to his political career, he added. But the voters clearly understood political corruption, and Bumpers's veto of a highly suspect political gambit solidified his role as the personification of the "new politics" in Arkansas, as Tom Sparks dubbed it. He and soon-to-be-president Jimmy Carter were the voices of the New South.

David Pryor
1975–1979

And Once Below a Time I Lordly Had the Trees and Leaves Trail with Daisies and Barley Down the Rivers of a Windfall Light.

—DYLAN THOMAS, "FERN HILL"

Arkansas is called the Natural State for good reason. Its abundant forests and wildlife accented by free-flowing streams and majestic mountain ranges make it a vacationer's paradise. Dale Bumpers, when he was governor, was wont to say, "Arkansas is a well-kept secret, and we want to keep it that way." Though economic development and enhanced business and agriculture opportunities are the mantra for any state "on the move," most Arkansans in their heart of hearts agree with Bumpers. Arkansans prefer to keep Arkansas pristine and *natural.*

After the catastrophic flood of the Mississippi River in 1927, Congress enacted the Flood Control Act of 1938, which authorized the U.S. Army Corps of Engineers to build dams for flood-control purposes and also to provide recreational lakes, a water source, and, in some cases, navigable waters and hydroelectric power.[1] The mission of the Corps was not necessarily malevolent.

David Pryor as governor. *Courtesy of Butler Center photos, Arkansas Studies Institute Collection, Little Rock.*

The trade-off, however, was the ruination of pristine waterways which for generations had been a source of recreational enjoyment. Those streams provided fishing and wading and swimming holes and pools. Thus, by the 1960s, destruction of these natural rivers began to raise an anguished cry from naturalists and preservationists comparable to that raised by the destruction of a Carnegie library or a Victorian residence. Corps activities gave rise to the "Keep Busy" slogan created by *Arkansas Gazette* cartoonist George Fisher as part of his campaign (and the *Arkansas Gazette*'s) against the Corps's damming natural streams and channelizing free-flowing rivers.[2]

In the 1960s and '70s in particular, the tension between the Corps of Engineers and preservationists evolved into open warfare. What gave some solace to the preservationists was that federal law required the states to bear part of the recreational costs associated with a new dam and related facilities. This, in effect, gave veto power to a governor who wished to block the project. Examples of the gubernatorial veto go back to the reign of Governor Orval Faubus, when he saved the Buffalo River from the Corps's Gilbert Dam project in 1965 at the urging of the newly formed Ozark Society. One need only cogitate on the hundreds of thousands of recreational hours enjoyed by floaters and fishermen that would have been lost had the Corps prevailed. Faubus vetoed the Corps project in a flowery and poetic letter to General William F. Cassidy of the Corps in Washington, D.C., on December 10, 1965. In doing so, he said: "The Buffalo River area is one of the greatest examples of the majesty of God's creation. The beauty of the region cannot be adequately described in any of the many languages of man."[3]

Next, there was Governor Dale Bumpers, whose efforts to save the Cache River and Bayou Deview from a Corps channelization project was heroic in its own right. Bumpers stood with the duck hunters and preservationists like Rex Hancock of Stuttgart against the rice farmers with sizeable farming operations who wanted the project for flood control and a regulated water source.

But no recent Corps project was as heated and controversial as the proposed Bell Foley Lake, which would result from damming the Strawberry River in north central Arkansas. This relatively small project was first authorized by the 1938 legislation. In 1970, however, the Corps announced that this dam project was next, and as David Pryor later put it, "The fat was in the fire."[4]

The Strawberry River has its origin just south of the Missouri line in Fulton County. It then meanders toward the southeast through Izard County, Sharp County, and Lawrence County until it merges with the Black River northeast of Batesville in Independence County. The dam proposed by the Corps was to be 410 feet high, and the lake would cover some 12,000 acres. The cost in 1975 was estimated at $43 million, but it was expected to climb to $100 million by 1978. Both the dam and the lake were to be named after Bell Foley, a man who had been a well-known and well-liked blacksmith in the Ozark foothills.[5]

Those advocating the project were major citizens, speculators, and developers in north central Arkansas who wanted a recreational lake in Sharp County and saw the Strawberry River as a minor, insignificant stream. Coming to their aid were significant players in the Arkansas congressional delegation: Senator John McClellan, Congressman Wilbur Mills, and Congressman Bill Alexander. The question was on which side would Governor David Pryor light?

Pryor had had other difficult issues during his first term as governor, which began in January 1975. There was a firefighters' strike in Pine Bluff, when he called out the National Guard to afford fire protection to the citizens of Pine Bluff and was called a strikebreaker by organized labor.[6] And there was his highly publicized support for the Equal Rights Amendment for women. To Pryor, calling out the National Guard had been a split-second decision and something of a no-brainer. As governor, he could not leave Pine Bluff at risk and unprotected. The political fallout, though, was heavy. The AFL-CIO endorsed Congressman Jim Guy Tucker three years later over Pryor in the race for the U.S. Senate seat vacated by the death of John McClellan. The Equal Rights Amendment, on the other hand, was a cultural issue in which Pryor fervently believed.

Now, as he took office in 1975, the Bell Foley Dam had landed squarely on his desk as an issue. Somehow Bumpers had "finessed" it for four years, but Pryor knew he no longer had that luxury. There were decent arguments on both sides, and Pryor was well aware that those arguments had to be studied, analyzed, and digested before a decision could be made. The proponents of each position were committed to their cause, which meant the political repercussions, either way he decided, would be real and pronounced.

At his core, Pryor is small-town Arkansas. He was born and raised in Camden on the Ouachita River, a town of small shops, three movie theaters, Christian values, Friday night football, and family security.[7] Edgar Pryor, his father, was owner of the Pryor Chevrolet dealership but had served as Ouachita County sheriff. His mother, Susan Newton Pryor, had run, unsuccessfully, for deputy circuit clerk but was something of a community activist for the underprivileged. The Ouachita River was integral to his childhood. Most summers, he spent his time fishing and swimming at Mustin Lake, which had been formed by the Ouachita River. While not the Mississippi River, he equates his childhood in some respects to the romantic life of a Tom Sawyer and a

Huckleberry Finn. It was most certainly a secure and carefree time in rural America.

But David Pryor has always been, first and foremost, a politician, whether it was as student leader in high school and college, representative and young Turk in the General Assembly in the early 1960s, or congressman from the Fourth Congressional District. Early on, he set his sights high—the U.S. Senate. But that was not to be, at least not in 1972. He lost a fierce runoff election to Senate incumbent John McClellan. It was a stunning defeat for the still young Pryor, and for a while he was at loose ends.

Political considerations, though, were never far from his mind, and in 1974, he announced for governor of the state after learning that Dale Bumpers would abandon that post and run for the U.S. Senate. His significant opponent would be the redoubtable Orval Faubus, who, yet again, was mounting a comeback effort.

Pryor defeated Faubus handily in the Democratic primary, and the symbolism of the race was lost on no one. Pryor, the rising star and beacon for the new South, administered the coup de grâce to the man who personified the sins of the past. For Faubus, it was the last hurrah. He had divorced his wife of thirty-eight years, Alta, in 1969 and married a somewhat meretricious and ambitious woman from New England, Elizabeth Westmoreland. His message in his last campaign sounded dated and an echo of yesteryear. He had his devotees, and Senator John McClellan, still smarting from his successful campaign against the upstart Pryor in 1972, no doubt sent support Faubus's way. But it was to no avail. Pryor beat Faubus and former Lieutenant Governor Bob Riley without a runoff. In his victory speech, the young governor-elect read a telegram sent to Mrs. Francis Cherry, which said "the score was settled."[8] It was a reference to Cherry's defeat by Orval Faubus twenty years earlier. Pryor later regretted what he termed "an unnecessary grandstand play."[9]

Now Pryor was about to be chief executive of the state at age forty-one, which was a role somewhat unfamiliar to him. By style and temperament, he was more suited to be a legislator and a lawmaker. What he had aspired to in 1972 in his run against McClellan was to join the most elite legislative club in the world, the U.S. Senate. He enjoyed the legislative camaraderie. Now he found himself, as the cliché has it, alone at the top.

The night before his inauguration in 1975, he sought advice from three predecessors as governor. Faubus told him that he hoped Pryor never had to deal with an execution as he, Faubus, had to do in the Emmett Earl Leggett matter. Leggett had been convicted of murdering a fourteen-year-old boy and received the death penalty. Faubus ultimately commuted Leggett's death sentence in 1957 in the middle of the Central High crisis.[10]

Dale Bumpers's advice was, "Be magnanimous."[11] That was the polestar that Pryor had adopted and hoped to follow. Bumpers added that he should not act "in haste" on important decisions.[12]

Sid McMath was of the same mind and noted that many times the popular thing to do at the moment is not the right thing to do.[13] Pryor would remember the wisdom of Bumpers and McMath as the battle over the Bell Foley Dam began to take shape on the horizon.

The National Guard's Huey helicopter banked slightly and descended so that Governor Pryor could get a closer look at the Strawberry River and the site for the proposed Bell Foley Dam. Pryor liked to get a firsthand view of problems he had to confront. It was true of the nursing home industry six years earlier when he went undercover in the Washington, D.C., area as a congressman to examine nursing home abuses. It was true in his early days as governor when he made a surprise nighttime visit to Cummins Penitentiary to see what the open-barrack conditions were really

George Fisher's take on the U.S. Corps of Engineers and the Strawberry River. *Published with permission of the* Arkansas Democrat-Gazette, *copyright January 22, 1975. Arkansas Arts Center Library Collection of George Fisher Cartoons.*

like. Now he wanted to see where the dam would be located and its effect.

With him, Pryor recalls, were Bruce Lindsey (now president of the Clinton Foundation), Joan Vehik (now chief assistant to his son, Senator Mark Pryor), and Bill Wilson (now U.S. district judge).[14] To his right in the helicopter sat staff assistant Joan Vehik. "Right below us will be a Dairy Queen and used car lot" if the dam is built, Pryor recalls her saying.[15] It had an impact on him.

But proponents of the dam made up of farmers and businessmen were upping the ante and pressuring Pryor for a pledge of $6 million in state revenues (roughly half of the recreation cost of the project) by April 1, 1975.[16] On March 20, 1975, when they met with Pryor, the legislature was currently in session, and several legislators supported the dam, including Senator Bill Walmsley of Batesville.

"All in the world that's behind this is a bunch of spectators," said one of the dam's opponents, Lester Clayton.[17] He spoke for the affected farmers and ecological groups. The point made was abundantly clear. Many proponents had an interest in the land bordering the lake to be, including farmer and Batesville bank owner E. R. Coleman, who headed up the proponents' association, and Congressman Bill Alexander. Both men had reportedly bought eighty acres on August 10, 1973, in some proximity to the proposed dam.[18] According to former state representative Earl T. Peebles of Hardy, who lived above the proposed dam site, "These people [the speculators] are stuck. There's no way they can get their money back without the dam."[19] But the proponents also made a good case for flood control, recreation, and economic enhancement, which included job opportunities on the lake as the result of the development.

Pryor did not make a decision by April 1, despite urgings for him to do so. Indeed, it was not until July 9, 1975, that he wrote Colonel Donald Weinert, the district engineer.[20] He began, in that letter, voicing the positive aspects of recreation and employment which would be fostered by the dam. Then he noted his concerns: the number of acres flooded (12,000) versus the acreage benefited (6,000), the "mud flats" surrounding the lake, and the "major problem" of obligating $6 to $8 million (half of the recreation cost) for the project in this "grave period of fiscal uncertainty and economic fluctuation." Finally, he cited the constitutional prohibition in the Arkansas Constitution against obligating funds for more than two years for a debt that had not been authorized by a vote of the people.

Pryor's principal objection, though, is best summed up in one paragraph of his letter to Colonel Weinert: "The damming of any natural and free flowing stream is an irreversible and ever enduring act. We should undertake such a step with only the strongest assurance that the environmental, ecological, and aesthetic quality of the area will not be impaired." A more prosaic sentiment was offered by dam opponent Mrs. Robie Hash: "I have drank it, fished in it, swam and played in it, and used water from it to wash my clothes. I love it as it is. I do not believe there is justification for such expenditure. Before God, I do not know how anyone can justify taking people's homes and lands that they have worked a lifetime to acquire."[21] Pryor, based on his Ouachita River experiences, heartily agreed.

Following his decision, as Pryor put it, "All hell broke loose!"[22] The *Arkansas Gazette* quoted the *Batesville Guard* that Pryor's decision "is apt to have damaging political repercussions for him" and that the support from residents in the more populated areas of Jonesboro, Batesville, and Walnut Ridge was "overwhelming."[23] It was reported from one Evening Shade resident who had sold 120 aces of river hilltop to two speculators that the men "went cross eyed" when they heard the news that the dam would not be built.[24] Congressman Bill Alexander quickly said he would continue to support the dam even after Pryor's letter, and Senator John McClellan said he did not agree with the decision.[25] But upstream farmers, ecological groups, and much of the state's press applauded the Pryor veto.

The issue of the Bell Foley Dam did not end with Pryor's letter. The proponents, and particularly the Bell Foley Dam Association, resolved to take the issue to the Arkansas General Assembly for legislation to overcome Pryor's constitutional problems related to obligating state funds for the future. Not surprisingly, the General Assembly adopted a resolution in January 1976 "expressing continuing interest" in the dam. The project still had a pulse.[26] But not for very long.

A year later on January 17, 1977, Pryor announced his opposition to legislation introduced by Representative Doug Adams of Strawberry and Representative John E. Miller of Melbourne authorizing State Parks and Tourism to agree to provide the state's one-half share of recreational costs, now estimated at $8 million.[27] Lake user fees, Miller maintained, could be used to defray the state appropriation. Pryor and State Parks and Tourism director Richard Davies specifically questioned the claim that the user fees would, in fact, offset the cost of the project. To do so, they claimed, the fees would have to be unusually high. In a public statement, Pryor added that it would be "irresponsible" to commit the state to a fifty-year payback obligation.[28]

But the grass fire had been lit, and the House of Representatives passed the bill overwhelmingly. Five days later, the Senate did the same, though ten senators refrained from voting.

In an innovative legislative maneuver, the Senate held up on releasing the bill for the governor's action, and the Bell Foley Dam Association commenced an advertising campaign to extol the benefits of the dam and to urge the public to voice its support to Pryor.[29] It was all to no avail. The Senate released the bill, and on February 3, 1977, Pryor vetoed it. In doing so, he repeated that it would be fiscally irresponsible for him to sign it.[30]

Throughout the debate over the Bell Foley Dam during David Pryor's first two years as governor, he displayed conscientiousness and thoughtfulness. Though he agonized at times, especially in the summer of 1975, Pryor is now comforted by the certain knowledge that time has proven him right. Nevertheless, in the short term, with his reelection taking place in 1976, his decision seemed unwise at best and disastrous at worst.

In 1978, Pryor stood for election once again for the U.S. Senate. This time, he faced two accomplished and talented challengers, both of whom were U.S. representatives—Ray Thornton and Jim Guy Tucker. He prevailed ultimately in a runoff election against Tucker, but the rancor generated from his Bell Foley decision was evident in the poll results. All of the counties directly impacted by his veto sided with his opponents, according to Pryor, who made a point of doing an analysis of the poll results after the election.[31]

Now, thirty-five years after the Bell Foley Dam decision, Pryor's intransigence on this issue continues to be applauded and appreciated. In April of 2009, at a conference held at Southern University in Magnolia by the Arkansas Historical Association to recognize those who had taken action to protect the environment, David Pryor was a principal speaker because of his work to save the Strawberry River. In his remarks, Pryor said: "Some of you have asked me, 'Where is the Strawberry River?' My answer is simple. It's where it has been for the last million years. It is still beautiful, it is still proud, it is still flowing free."[32]

Frank White
1981–1983

But be ye doers of the word, and not hearers only, deceiving your own selves . . . , but a doer of the work, this man shall be blessed in his deed.

—JAMES 1:22, 25, KING JAMES BIBLE

To Governor Frank White, the issue was an easy one. "Hey, it's fair," you could hear him say. "You teach evolution, you teach creation science." Reduced down to a question of balanced teaching and a structural, managerial approach, White was at ease with his commitment to allow both to be taught in the public schools. The commitment had been made after his campaign against incumbent Bill Clinton and during his early days as governor. He knew that a creation-science bill providing that both would be taught had fervent support, especially with certain Christians in northwestern Arkansas but, in truth, throughout the state. White saw no problem with it.

Frank White was a born-again Christian, largely due to his devout second wife, Gay Daniels White, whom he married in 1975 and who brought him into the fold. In a 1981 interview, Gay White explained: "God has used me in Frank's life. . . . Frank

Frank White, 1982. *Personal photograph of his widow, Gay White.*

tried my approach to life and found it appealing. . . . He knows now God loves him. . . . He reads the Bible and believes it is the word of God."[1]

White was more than willing to be saved. The Christianity practiced at Gay's church, Fellowship Bible in Little Rock, a non-denominational church, gave him a strict creed and routine to follow. Each day, he and Gay prayed together and read scripture.[2] His faith became the center and most important thing in his life.

Hence, it was no surprise that on election night, November 4, 1980, when he declared victory over Bill Clinton, he announced it was "a victory for the Lord."[3] Heartfelt, steadfast, and sincere, the statement typified the ebullient, boisterous, and blunt Frank White, who spoke often without a full understanding of the potential fallout from his words or how his statement might be received. His widow, Gay, now says White was too honest and candid to be a politician. He had too much integrity, she says.[4] Nevertheless, his "victory" statement illustrated how once he accepted the faith, he did not hesitate to voice his beliefs for all "with ears to hear." He found that he would spend the next three months explaining what he meant by his "victory" comment.

It was apparently during his campaign against Bill Clinton in 1980 that he was first approached by his friend and campaign worker Carl Hunt to support a creation-science bill that mandated equal time for teaching creation science so long as evolution was taught.[5] Evolution was easily defined, dating back to Charles Darwin's *Origin of the Species,* first published in 1859, setting forth the doctrine of natural selection. The creationists advanced a more instantaneous creation rather than one that evolved over millions of years and, according to some, one more akin to the Genesis depiction of a six-day event. White agreed that equal time should be afforded to both evolution and creation science. A model bill developed by the Creation Science Research Center, which provided that creation science be taught if evolutionary science was taught, was quickly introduced in the 1981 regular session of the General Assembly.

The bill, Senate Bill 482, was sponsored by Senator Jim Holsted of Little Rock, a supporter of creationism, and passed the Senate by a hasty vote of twenty-two to two. In the House, Representative Cliff Hoofman knew his obligation was to shepherd the bill of Senator Holsted, who was "his senator," through that body. He did so, and the bill passed the House by a vote of sixty-nine to eighteen. It now sat before Frank White on his desk. It was not a lengthy piece of legislation—only six pages. What it did was define evolutionary science and creation science and call for a balanced approach to teaching both "sciences." It specifically stated in the body of the bill that the legislation in no wise should be deemed a mandate for the teaching of religion.

As Frank White gazed down at the bill, he knew the moment of truth had arrived. His legal aides, Bill Bethea and Linda Garner, had told him about the bill, and he was well aware that the bill was not without controversy. Much had been written about it already, not only in Arkansas but in other states as well. It would be the first act in the country mandating equal time for creation science if evolution was taught. That historic groundbreaking event appealed to White. Plus, he had told the sponsors of the bill as well as the bill's supporters that he would sign it. And Frank White, to his core, was a handshake businessman. A commitment in business and government meant something.

White was a Texan by birth, whose role model, if not by design, was unmistakably another Texan, Lyndon Baines Johnson. Both men were big, overpowering, volcanic, and truly larger than life.

To make a point, White, like Johnson, would get up close to his "victim" face-to-face and cup his elbow as he talked. And like Johnson, White liked to win—at everything—from backgammon to political campaigns.

His life experiences before assuming the governorship would have steeled him more for a business career than one as a policy maker. He was educated at the Naval Academy and did his five-year stint in the U.S. Air Force, where he flew missions around the world. Returning to Little Rock with his first wife, Mary Blue Hollenberg, a native, he worked at a brokerage firm, a bank, as director of the Arkansas Industrial Development Commission, as part of Governor David Pryor's administration, and then as president of a savings-and-loan association. He was now forty-seven and the savings-and-loan job appeared to be in jeopardy. He decided to opt for a political race against the young and somewhat immature Bill Clinton, who had mixed reviews during his first term as governor.

White had always had political aspirations, said close friends at the time.[6] And White agreed, although his first choice in politics was a race for Congress. The public schools in Washington, though, were a definite minus for him. And Bill Clinton was vulnerable after a skein of mistakes in office due in part to his ineptitude and in part to a politically inept staff. White announced for governor.

His public relations man for the political campaign, Craig Rains, described White as a "genius," but his acquaintances also saw in him a tendency to bully and be overbearing.[7] After his election, some legislators agreed with that assessment.[8] Preston Bynum, his executive secretary while governor, explains that White "was partially deaf, and his deafness caused him to speak loudly," which seemed like blustering.[9] White could also be very funny and ingratiating. That, his military experience, and his man's-man persona stood him in good stead with the electorate.

What won the campaign for him against Bill Clinton in 1980, however, were three political ads on television that are generally considered among the best ever produced in Arkansas. The first ad illustrated Clinton's increase in state-assessed fees for car tags.[10] As each dollar increase was counted off in the ad, it was accompanied by a cash register's ring. There were multiple rings. The second ad showed a taxpayer burying silver dollars in a crop row to lampoon Clinton's high-priced program to train workers on how to saw wood. The third, and without question the most potent, was an ad showing black Cubans rioting at Fort Chaffee outside of Fort Smith, after Clinton was persuaded by President Jimmy Carter to incarcerate the Cuban felons Castro had sent to the United States in Arkansas. The combined message was clear. Clinton had not stood up to Jimmy Carter, and Arkansas had suffered. Frank White on the other hand—a business man, hunter, and navy pilot—was fit for the job. He shocked the world when he defeated Bill Clinton, who was already being bruited about as presidential timber.

White, though, while a businessman and skilled administrator, was severely lacking in one respect where Clinton would not have been. This deficiency was in not fully appreciating the emotional response to allowing creationism to be taught in the classroom. In a sense, White had a tin ear to the significance of the issue. Open warfare over evolution did not begin with Charles Darwin or with the Great Awakening for devout Christians in rural America in the nineteenth century or with the fabled Scopes "Monkey" trial in Dayton, Tennessee, over the teaching of evolution in 1925. The creation of the world and man's emergence have been debated since the beginning of time. Yet, evolution, the Great Awakening, and the Scopes trial all had dramatic repercussions throughout the country and particularly in White's adopted state.

Arkansas had had its own anti-evolution law stemming from the Great Awakening, and that law was struck down as unconstitutional by the U.S. Supreme Court in the landmark case of *Epperson v. Arkansas* in 1968.[11] The Arkansas Supreme Court had heard the *Epperson* case first and had been so fearful of the political consequences of ruling the act unconstitutional that it refused, in a two-sentence opinion, to consider the constitutional issue on the merits.[12] The U.S. Supreme Court was of a different mind and voided the Arkansas act as an establishment of religion in violation of the First Amendment. Since *Epperson,* anti-evolution proponents had sought other avenues to abate the chilling effect of that decision, and creation-science legislation was one such avenue. On the other side of the issue, there were those who chafed under the potential embarrassment of Arkansas being viewed, yet again, as an unsophisticated, fundamentalist state that persisted in attacking evolution on religious grounds.

Senate Bill 482 did little to abate the notion that science and religion would be pitted against each other in the classroom. The definitions of "creation science" and "evolution science" in the bill were revealing, especially as they referenced man's ancestry from the apes:

> (a) "Creation-science" means the scientific evidences for creation and inferences from those scientific evidences. Creation-science includes the scientific evidences and related inferences that indicate: (1) Sudden creation of the universe, energy, and life from nothing; (2) The insufficiency of mutation and natural selection in bringing about development of all living kinds from a single organism;

> (3) Changes only within fixed limits of originally created kinds of plants and animals; (4) Separate ancestry for man and apes; (5) Explanation of the earth's geology by catastrophism, including the occurrence of a worldwide flood; and (6) A relatively recent inception of the earth and living kinds.
>
> (b) "Evolution-science" means the scientific evidences for evolution and inferences from those scientific evidences. Evolution-science includes the scientific evidences and related inferences that indicate: (1) Emergence by naturalistic processes of the universe from disordered matter and emergence of life from nonlife; (2) The sufficiency of mutation and natural selection in bringing about development of present living kinds from simple earlier kinds; (3) Emergence by mutation and natural selection of present living kinds from simple earlier kinds; (4) Emergence of man from a common ancestor with apes; (5) Explanation of the earth's geology and the evolutionary sequence by uniformitarianism; and (6) An inception several billion years ago of the earth and somewhat later of life.[13]

The lines between evolution and creation science were clearly drawn by the legislature, and to White, giving both an equal platform in public education was entirely appropriate. Plus, he had committed to support the concept. Against this historic backdrop, he signed the creation-science bill into law, which immediately brought into focus the constitutional issue of whether creation science was truly science or, in fact, religion. White may have anticipated that, but he did not anticipate the rancor and furor that would arise over his signing a bill that was inherently fraught with controversy. Exacerbating the situation was the fact that after he signed it, he made the fatal admission that he had not read the bill in its entirety or evaluated each section. This only fueled the outcry from creation-science opponents, who viewed it all as a subterfuge to teach Genesis in the public schools.

George Fisher's celebrated comment on creation science. *Published with permission of the* Arkansas Democrat-Gazette, *copyright March 19, 1981. Arkansas Arts Center Library Collection of George Fisher Cartoons.*

The story in the *Arkansas Gazette* the day after White's signing trumpeted this headline: "He Hasn't Read It But White Signs Bill on 'Creation.'"[14] The body of the story gave White's assessment of the bill: "Mr. White says he knows very little about the concept of evolution or the 'creation-science' theory and that he doesn't accept either one, but that he agreed both should be taught. He said he is a Christian who believes in the Bible, but he asked rhetorically, 'What does God and religion have to do with creation-science?' He said they weren't related and that 'creation-science' could be taught without teaching a religious creed."[15]

Ten days later, White and Gay, his wife, gave their religious "testimony" at Heritage Baptist Temple in Little Rock. The resulting article in the *Arkansas Gazette* included White's comments about the adverse reaction to the creation-science act. He said there had been "great national acclaim about the stupidity of the governor of Arkansas who signed a bill to require the teaching of creation science equal with evolution science. I can't tell you the hostility of the letters that have come from all over the nation, of the subjecting of abuse because of my consideration that creation-science even has any credibility."[16]

White also told the congregation, "I believe in Genesis. I believe in the scriptures. [But] there's not one word in the bill that requires the teaching of a religious creed, doctrine or God." He said criticism of the measure is through ignorance and added, "And it brings the thought to me [that] perhaps the outcry is but that of an uninformed society who doesn't realize that this is the truth and the light."[17]

According to then state representative Cliff Hoofman, who handled Senate Bill 482 in the House and who is now a state highway commissioner, the governor was criticized for not reading or studying the bill, "but the whole darn legislature should have been blamed. Nobody read it. There was no debate or discussion of the bill in committee or on the House floor. There was no discussion about whether it was right or wrong. The potential impact was not known. It was never discussed on the merits."[18]

Hoofman said that Senator Holsted had given him books to read on creation science, and he had boned up on it. Yet, as he was prepared to speak in the House committee, a motion was made to pass the bill, which succeeded. On the House floor, he had started down to the podium to speak on the bill when Representative Jodie Mahony from El Dorado moved the House to send the bill back to committee in an effort to kill it. That motion was unsuccessful. What did succeed was an immediate motion to vote on the bill, which passed. The subsequent vote on the bill itself also succeeded. "The true story about the creation-science bill," says Hoofman, "is it was all done procedurally."[19] Not only had the governor committed on the bill, but it was obvious to Hoofman that many House members had too. They did not want to become embroiled in debate over the bill on the House floor.

For the next several weeks after Senate Bill 482 was signed into law as Act 590, White and his staff sparred with Joan Vehik, the bill clerk for White and governors dating back to Dale Bumpers. The issue was whether White had indeed been briefed on the bill by his staff attorneys outside of her presence. Vehik, who admitted she opposed the bill on philosophical grounds, questioned whether he had been briefed and further revealed that she had met with White before he signed the bill in an effort to dissuade him from signing it. He shrugged her off "in a sort of humorous way," according to news accounts.[20] To Vehik, it seemed White had committed to someone to sign the bill, and in his mind that ended the matter. Vehik added that White told her that Arkansas would receive national attention as the first state to enact such a law. Vehik responded that the national attention would not be that favorable.[21]

Vehik proved prescient. Act 590 was immediately viewed by opponents as an effort to teach religion and the Genesis story in the public schools in direct contravention of the Establishment Clause of the First Amendment. A lawsuit was later filed in federal district court in Little Rock by the American Civil Liberties Union; and the federal district judge, William Overton, ruled, after a two-week trial, that creation science was not science but religion and that the act was unconstitutional (*McLean v. Arkansas Board of Education*, 1982).[22] In the appeal of a similar case striking down a comparable creation-science law in Louisiana, the U.S. Supreme Court ruled that the legislation was unconstitutional (*Edwards v. Aguillard*, 1987).[23] Two Supreme Court justices, however, dissented in the *Edwards* case on grounds of a secular purpose—Chief Justice William Rehnquist and Justice Antonin Scalia. The dissenters argued that creation science, under the principle of academic freedom, could be given equal time in the classroom and still pass constitutional muster.

Frank White maintained later, as he ended his two-year term as governor, that one of his real mistakes in office was the way he handled the aftermath of the creation-science enactment, including his admission that he signed the bill without reading all of its provisions.[24] In truth, however, his lapse in that regard was not unusual. Many governors sign bills into law without reading every word, as Vehik herself noted. They are briefed on the contents by bill clerks and staff. Few governors, however, *admit* they were not aware of everything a bill does. Plus, even though they may not have read every word, they are usually intimately familiar with the salient features of the bill. White, when asked, was not familiar with some of the act's terms, such as the explicit statement that creation science is not religion. Again, White's naiveté and failure to correctly navigate the Charybdis and Scylla through which he was sailing proved his undoing.

Without question, White's signing of Act 590 was the defining moment of his two-year term. Henceforth, one political cartoonist, George Fisher for the *Arkansas Gazette,* always drew him with a peeled banana in his hand in reference to Darwin's theorizing that man descended from the apes. It undoubtedly cost White the election in 1982, when Bill Clinton, now contrite, more mature, and less zealous, ousted him in a well-orchestrated comeback campaign that began with Clinton's apology to the people of Arkansas for his marred first term.

What does this tell us about Frank White? Surely his signing of Act 590 does not exhibit great courage, though it might evidence his perception of fairness by giving equal time to evolution and creationism and his deep-seated religious convictions. No doubt, he believed in what he was doing, in authorizing conflicting views on creation. But he appeared disingenuous when he said that he was not attuned to the fact that some might consider creation science as a backdoor vehicle for teaching Genesis. Surely, he must have had some inkling that creation science, if taught, would arguably be viewed as religion and as a breach in the wall of separation between church and state. That is what the Supreme Court ultimately held in its decision on the issue—that creation science was not science but religion. White, though, was willing to take that risk.

Frank White did do some good things for the state, which Preston Bynum is quick to point out, as is White's widow, Gay.[25] He reduced the car tag cost and removed the Cubans from Fort Chaffee. His pay increases for teachers and state employees, foreign trade successes, and his work for job training and home and rural health care were also accomplishments of note. Gay says today that White "did not get a fair shake" from the press during the creation science debate.[26] He was "too candid," she says.[27]

But when confronted with an issue of enormous and far-reaching significance, which is what the creation science/evolution debate was, White fell victim to what was presented to him as an easy solution to the perceived inequity of teaching Darwinism in our public schools. In refusing to plumb the depths of the issue and in hastily signing Act 590 into law, he blurred his state role with his religious beliefs. In the process, he sacrificed his political career. The result is that Arkansas now has figured prominently in two anti-evolution skirmishes that have led to two landmark decisions from the U.S. Supreme Court, one which supported the teaching of evolution and the other which rejected the teaching of religious faith as an alternative to Darwinism.

Bill Clinton

1979–1981
1983–1992

While we can take justifiable pride in what our schools and colleges have historically accomplished and contributed to the United States and the well being of its people, the educational foundations of our society are being eroded by a rising tide of mediocrity that threatens our very future as a Nation and a people.

—A NATION AT RISK, APRIL 1983

Bill Clinton leaned back in his chair and stuck his long legs under his desk. With his left elbow propped against the arm of his chair, he placed his thumb under his chin and extended his forefinger along the side of his face. Thus supported, he watched his wife, Hillary, and his chief of staff, Betsy Wright, debate the politics of education in his office. We took a hell of a big step forward in education reform two years ago, he thought as he watched. Before then we were dead last in per capita education spending. New teachers now had to take the national certification exam, a

Bill Clinton as governor. *Courtesy of Butler Center photos, Arkansas Studies Institute Collection, Little Rock.*

gifted-and-talented program was in place, and the Governor's School for exceptional students was started. There were also teacher pay increases, elementary school counselors were added, and education through age sixteen was mandated. But there were two areas that gnawed at him as he mused on the issue, areas where he had not been successful. There had been no enhanced public school funding, and consolidation of the state's 369 school districts was still off limits.[1]

Arkansas will never amount to a tinker's damn if we don't do something in both areas, he thought, as the two women argued their views. If the Arkansas Supreme Court rules our funding system for schools unconstitutional, it will be our one big chance to go for broke in education. For some students, you can throw them against the wall, and they will still make it because of their intelligence, drive, and self-esteem. For others, you have to put the corn where the hogs can get at it. We need a system that works for everybody.

He then spoke up. Education has to be the legislative focal point this year. They immediately agreed. All three knew how Arkansas always fared poorly in education rankings—either at or near the bottom. In four months, they would all learn how poorly the country as a whole fared in international rankings from a report prepared by President Ronald Reagan's Commission on Education, styled *A Nation at Risk.* Clinton later said after reading the report that if the nation as a whole was in such foul shape, Arkansas's education system "had to be on life support."[2]

The two women continued to talk education policy with great animation. This was really Hillary's passion, he thought. She knew the pitfalls in Arkansas as well as anyone in the state. Who better to spearhead a committee to overhaul the state's system and develop mandatory standards on a core curriculum to be taught, assessment of student achievement, and teacher competency that every school district had to meet? He would have to have legislative action establishing the committee, but he knew he could get this done. Yes, she would be perfect, he thought.

After winning reelection to the governorship in November 1982, having avenged the defeat by Frank White two years earlier, Bill Clinton was no longer thought to be the daring risk-taker he had been in his first term. Close friends now said he had been emasculated by the defeat and had "rabbit" blood. It was a clear reference to his perceived timidity. There was no question that he was different. Hillary described him as "humbler" and "more seasoned."[3] The Frank White upset in 1980 had been a body blow and certainly had derailed his meteoric political career, at least temporarily. He had every reason to be cautious and more circumspect now. But timidity had never been his strong suit.

There was also the distinct possibility that he might get political cover for his education reforms. Working its way to the Arkansas Supreme Court was a trial-court decision ruling that the school-funding system discriminated against poorer school districts and, thus, violated the state constitution. If that decision was affirmed by the Arkansas Supreme Court, a wholesale restructuring of the school-financing formula would be required.

On May 31, 1983, Clinton got his wish. The Arkansas Supreme Court affirmed the lower court's ruling in the case of *Dupree v. Alma School District* and held Arkansas's formula for funding state education unconstitutional.[4] Now he had no choice. He had to equalize per pupil expenditures for students in the poorer school districts to the level of funds available to students in the wealthier school districts. This meant either reducing funding for the wealthier districts or raising additional state money to bring the poorer districts in line. The Arkansas Supreme Court had been very clear about one point—the poor land wealth of a school district, which resulted in less school tax revenue for that district, could no longer determine the quality of a student's education within that district. That system was a thing of the past. The court decision "gave us an opportunity to do what we ought to do anyway," Clinton recollects today.[5]

When the General Assembly met in regular session in 1983, it passed the necessary legislation to authorize the Education Standards Committee, but Hillary Clinton did not want to chair it, at least not initially.[6] Later, she reluctantly agreed, and in the late spring/early summer of 1983, she and her committee were unleashed on the state. To amass the necessary information, she traveled to each of Arkansas's seventy-five counties, garnering comments, information, and recommendations on education reform. Armed with this data, Bill Clinton went on statewide television and advocated a one-cent increase in the sales tax to fund equality in education, a boost in the severance tax on natural gas to do the same, and the adoption of first-class education standards, including a core curriculum for every student. To succeed in his appeal, he knew he had to play on the state's deep-seated inferiority. "We are last in spending per child, teacher salaries, and total state and local taxes per person,"[7] he said. He had hit a raw nerve, and the positive reception in the state was palpable.

What he advanced in his talk were standards that included mandatory kindergartens; mandatory class size; mandatory eighth-grade testing; an enhanced curriculum in math, English, science, history, and social studies; a longer school year; and an improved opportunity for gifted-and-talented students.[8] His proposals far exceeded what President Reagan's commission had championed in *A Nation at Risk.*

Clinton, though, added a startling new wrinkle in his television address. To the surprise of everyone, his standards also famously mandated that existing teachers pass a National Teacher Examination in 1984, which would be a basic skills test in literacy, math, and science and which would be a condition for allowing teachers to continue to be certified to teach. What Hillary Clinton had found on the road was that many teachers were thought not to have these basic skills. Clinton himself had attended a few of those sessions, he says now, and heard the complaints about teacher lapses in basic skills. For example, he recalls seeing "one twenty-two word note with three misspelled words." Representative Julian Streett had also talked to him about the problem and showed him examples. "We had empirical evidence to support what I was proposing." he says. "We were not testing for an Einstein or Descartes, only basic skills."[9]

This was kerosene on the fire in the eyes of the Arkansas Education Association (AEA), the teachers' union. To the union, Bill Clinton had insulted Arkansas's teachers and thrown them under the bus. From the beginning, the union bitterly opposed teacher testing and vowed to fight it tooth and fang. At the same time, on September 21, 1983, almost seventy teachers at Central High School, in counterpoint to the AEA's opposition, signed a letter to Clinton supporting his education program, including testing, "to restore public confidence in the teaching profession." The teachers called for "meaningful school consolidation" and an "adequate curriculum."[10]

The war on teacher testing began with harsh words. Clinton labeled the teachers' union as "hysterical" about the issue. The union replied that Clinton's plan to test teachers was "insulting," "morally unjust," and a "cop out."[11] Arkansas NAACP president and state senator Jerry Jewell termed the test "racist," and yet certain African American leaders, according to Clinton, like Dr. Vic Hackley, chancellor of the University of Arkansas at Pine Bluff, supported standards and teacher testing.[12] The stage was set for a dramatic political struggle, rivaling any legislative dispute in Arkansas history.

The pivotal question now was whether Bill Clinton would stick by his guns and persevere with teacher testing? The Arkansas Supreme Court had not specifically required it in the *Dupree* decision. Would Clinton cave in on this critical point? Surely, according to Sam Bratton, who drafted the teacher-testing legislation and lobbied hard for its passage, neither he nor the Clintons were prepared for the vitriolic criticism and the truculence of the teachers' union.[13]

On October 3, 1983, Bill Clinton issued an amended proclamation, which called the General Assembly into special session to address his education standards. He included sixty items in his call, but his proposal on teacher testing was easily the most controversial. It read: "To require all teachers and administrators employed in the public schools of Arkansas to demonstrate competence by successful completion of a testing program including a test of subject content in the area of certification; to withhold recertification of teachers and administrators who do not demonstrate competence in functional academic skills and subject content in the area of certification."[14]

Representative Jodie Mahony of El Dorado introduced the testing bill (HB47) on October 10, 1983. It required teachers who wanted to be recertified to pass a basic skills test in reading, writing, and mathematics by June 1, 1987. This would give teachers three chances to pass it. The teachers also had to pass a test in the subject they taught or take college courses in that area. For the next

Bill Clinton tackles teacher testing. *Published with permission of the* Arkansas Democrat-Gazette, *copyright September 22, 1983. Published with permission of Jon Kennedy.*

thirty-one days of the special session, the debate over teacher testing in both houses was more than heated—it was explosive. After the special session, several esteemed legislators, like Henry Hodges of Little Rock, elected not to run again. The demands on their time caused by the regular session (the General Assembly had already met in regular session for more than sixty days in 1983) and the special session in October and November cut too deeply into their regular jobs and income.

Bill Clinton forged ahead. He was committed to fundamental education reform, and he knew that reform began with the teachers. He had always hungered for knowledge and was convinced that education was the great equalizer. His success proved the point. His passion is illustrated in his autobiography, *My Life*, and other biographies where influential teachers and their subjects are discussed. Shakespeare's plays like *Macbeth* and *Julius Caesar* are consistently selected for special mention, as is Cicero's denunciation of Cataline, covered in his Latin III class. Clinton opted to play the role of the defendant, Cataline, before his class because it was more of a challenge. In Clinton's mind, education was not something to be trivialized or marginalized. It was the road out of mediocrity.

AEA president Peggy Nabors appreciated this in Bill Clinton and knew he fervently believed that hard work in school during a student's formative years could take that student over the rainbow. It had certainly worked for Clinton. But in Nabors's estimation, Clinton's zeal for teacher testing was not only motivated by a yearning to weed out teachers who did not have a functional skill set in reading, writing, and mathematics. She believes to this day that a tinge of revenge colored Clinton's fervor for the testing issue.[15]

In his runoff campaign in the Democratic primary in 1982 against Joe Purcell, the AEA endorsed Bill Clinton, but its spokesman publicly said at the time that it was a "lukewarm" endorsement.[16] This was due in part to the AEA's perception that Clinton had failed to support an initiated act to implement education standards in 1981. The act failed by a very small percentage. Nabors is certain that Hillary in particular was "really ticked" by the "lukewarm" comment, and word had filtered back to her that Hillary had said to a group at the mansion she wanted "a piece of the AEA's ass."[17]

Despite the AEA's misgivings, it is hard to accept that revenge was a motivating factor for the Clintons' unwavering support of teacher testing. Former state representative David Malone of

Fayetteville, who sponsored an AEA bill for periodic teacher evaluations as an alternative to testing, believes the testing bill was more of a "political maneuver" to get the one-cent sales tax passed for higher educational standards. Teacher testing was a "sideline" issue but got all the attention, Malone says. He adds, "I thought he [Clinton] didn't have to do it to get the one cent passed. It would have passed without it."[18]

Two weeks into the special session, the *Arkansas Gazette* reported that the teacher-testing bill "[was] in serious trouble."[19] The *Gazette* added that many of the House Education Committee members were hostile and that it would be difficult for the bill to win the eleven committee votes necessary for a favorable recommendation. The next day, the paper reported that after another day of debate, it predicted a dark future for the bill and said, if anything, "the teacher-testing bill (HB 47) may have slipped a little further" and "it appears more and more that [Mr. Clinton will] have to compromise on it or suffer defeat."[20]

Odd alignments were being formed on both sides of the bill. "The AEA had scared the living daylights out of the legislators," Clinton now recollects;[21] and in an opposition bill sponsored by Representative Malone, the teachers' union was united with legislators and school superintendents who had been hostile to the AEA in the past. On the other side, there were legislators who frequently supported the AEA but who now endorsed the teacher-testing bill.

Senator Cliff Hoofman, who sponsored the testing bill in the Senate, now says the teacher's union got it wrong. They said it was "insulting" to have a test decide if you should qualify to be a teacher. "But the point was, if you couldn't pass the test you damn well weren't qualified to be in the classroom."[22] That subtle distinction was clearly lost on the AEA. The retort of Ermalee Boice of the AEA was that the bill would "single out Arkansas as the only state that believes its teachers are so bad, they have to pass a literacy test."[23]

In a dramatic maneuver, Hillary Clinton appeared before a joint session of the House and Senate of the General Assembly as chair of the Education Standards Committee at the beginning of the special session and advised the body on the pitiful state of Arkansas education and what needed to be done about it. Her speech was so persuasive and articulate that it prompted formidable House member Lloyd George to comment, "Well, fellas, it looks like we might have elected the wrong Clinton governor."[24] Plus, the Arkansas people wanted better education for their children, and the Arkansas Supreme Court had mandated equal education regardless of a school district's wealth. This would cost more money, and Clinton had proposed a one-cent increase in the sales tax to fund the increase.

Increasing taxes is never popular with the General Assembly. Yet, several bell cows in the House, Representative John Miller is an example, supported a resolution to only support the tax increase *if* the teacher-testing bill passed.[25] On the other hand, the full wrath of the AEA was descending on legislators who supported teacher testing, and African American leaders, fearful that the bill would affect black teachers disproportionately, closed ranks against the bill.[26]

Sam Bratton today admits that he had second thoughts about the teacher-testing bill in the wake of the volcanic reaction to the proposal, but he says the Clintons never wavered.[27] They may have been startled by the intensity of the furor, particularly on the part of the AEA, but by the end of October, after giving their full support to the bill, they were too far down the road to change their minds. Bill sponsor Representative Jodie Mahony agreed that the Clintons showed a lot of starch in the face of the controversy. "It was intense," he says. "They didn't flinch or waver."[28]

It was during this time that Clinton employed his shuttle advocacy, for which he became famous, to the fullest. Racing back and forth between the House and Senate chambers, a tactic that was unusual for governors until Clinton, he lobbied for testing and his tax package and against certain amendments. His personal appearances, arm twisting, and dealing, while resented by some, paid large dividends.

The dam finally broke in the House, and the testing bill passed on October 27, 1983, by a vote of fifty-seven to twenty-eight. But once the bill reached the Senate, it was met with an AEA-supported filibuster. That is when Bill Clinton did a "Hail Mary pass," as he now puts it.[29] He called a press conference and announced, "There will be no tax without a testing bill," and he vowed to veto his own sales-tax increase if the teacher-testing bill did not pass.[30] It was a scorched-earth strategy. Clinton was fully aware that without the additional sales tax, there would be no teacher raises, no new standards for school districts, and no new constitutional school-funding formula. It was a risky gamble, but it succeeded.

"Hallelujah!" Clinton cried and slapped his desk hard when he heard that the Senate had just approved the House version of the testing bill.[31] It was Halloween Day, an irony that was not lost on the AEA and especially not on its president, Peggy Nabors. Criticism of teacher testing and of Clinton proliferated after the bill passed. Senator John Lisle of Springdale, a member of the Senate Education Committee, said, "I am not convinced that we are doing anything really remarkable for education."[32] Terry Humble of Harrison added in an op ed piece in the *Arkansas Gazette* that was laced with sarcasm, "I regret that I was so incompetent when her [Hillary Clinton's] husband was a student in my school."[33]

Clinton signed the teacher-testing bill as Act 76 on Monday, November 7, 1983, amid great hoopla. He referred to the bill as "very progressive and a very positive part of our education program."[34] The testing wars, however, would continue. Ermalee Boice addressed three hundred teachers at the AEA convention in Little Rock and said, "The governor may have won this battle in the war against teachers, but this is a war we will not lose."[35]

Clinton was resolute. At a speech to a group of retired teachers, he gave some insight into why he proposed the testing bill: "I proposed it in response to complaints made in unsolicited letters and statements made at public hearings of Hillary's Education Standards Committee. . . . I became genuinely concerned by the lack of public support, the skepticism the public seems to feel about what ought to be the most exacting profession we have." He added that the tests "will show the overwhelming majority of our teachers are well-prepared to do the job they have [been] hired on to do, and that will bolster public support."[36]

Yet the impact teacher testing was having on his political future was never far from Clinton's mind. In a November 19, 1983, television interview with a KATV reporter in Little Rock, Clinton "said he had no idea what the 'political toll' would be for his strong advocacy of the law" and remarked, "I just know that I believed very, very strongly in the bill. I think we couldn't have passed the sales tax without it. My only concern has been to ask, 'Is this good for the children?' and if the answer is yes, then the political consequences should be put aside."[37]

By now the issue had become one of national interest. In a January 24, 1984, appearance on NBC's *Today* show, Clinton debated the teacher-testing bill with AEA president Peggy Nabors. Waving his index finger, he said, "There are a small but not insignificant number of teachers who lack the adequacy of basic skills that every teacher should have and who should be required to improve those basic skills if they're going to remain in the classroom."[38] When National Education Association members asked Clinton in a panel discussion three days later what basis he had for claiming that there were incompetent teachers in his state, he "cited letters he'd received from parents and teachers," which evidenced again that the bill was prompted by concerns voiced by the public to Hillary's Standards Committee.[39]

Two developments then surfaced which showed the testing issue was far from dead. The National Education Association called for the teacher-testing bill to be repealed by the General Assembly. Clinton answered on March 30, 1984, and said, "We need to be able to say with confidence that we are going to have as modern, as adequate, as sensible an approach to our teacher education program as exists anywhere."[40] The AEA responded by announcing that ten public school teachers had filed a lawsuit challenging the constitutionality of the teacher-testing law in Pulaski County Chancery Court.[41]

The foray against the testing law was initially successful. On February 21, 1985, the House of Representatives voted to repeal the teacher-testing act. Clinton vowed to veto any repeal of the act and went to the airwaves to inform the public that the teacher-testing bill was under fierce attack. His radio ads gave listeners telephone numbers for their legislators, and the gambit paid off. The public quickly made known their support for teacher testing. After one week, the *Gazette* reported that "the switchboard at the capitol was bombarded with calls" against the repeal.[42] The Senate killed the bill to repeal on March 5, 1985. Other efforts to water down Act 76 in the 1985 legislative session met a similar fate.

Clinton won on the second front as well. Seventeen days later, Chancellor Bruce T. Bullion declared that the teacher-testing law was constitutional. Specifically, Bullion rejected the teachers' claim that the act violated the Equal Protection provisions of the Arkansas Constitution by requiring certified personnel who were employed in Arkansas public schools in the 1984–1985 school year to take the tests and by not requiring teachers who were on a leave of absence or were not working at a public school to take the test. The final obstacle to teacher testing had been removed.

But a critical issue remained. What entity would administer the test and how would the questions to test teachers be formulated? The first testing company contacted was the same company that administered the basic-skills test to new teachers. The NEA opposed its involvement, and it backed off. The test was ultimately administered on March 24, 1985, by Instructional Objective Exchange Assessment Associates (IOX), a California company, which entered into an agreement with the state to administer the test at a cost of $284,995.[43] The test eventually would be composed of multiple-choice questions on reading and math and a required two-hundred-word writing sample.

The degree of the test's difficulty was the real stumbling block. A pilot test had been given to a limited pool of teachers statewide, and the failure percentages that came back were "way too high," according to Sam Bratton; perhaps as high as 50 percent.[44] And African American teachers fared far worse than whites.

At a meeting held at Representative Gloria Cabe's house after the pilot test, the Clintons, Cabe, Betsy Wright, and Bratton attended.[45] They decided that the test would have to be made easier, though all in the room recognized this as a "dumbing down" maneuver. A 50 percent failure rate on the other hand would be intolerable and unsupportable politically, and black teachers had fared worse on the field test. Adjustments to the test had to be made.

Throughout the firefight over the testing bill and the aftermath with the test itself, the ultra-pragmatic strategist Dick Morris was advising Clinton.[46] Morris was admittedly effective, but the question was asked, At what price? Sam Bratton would later say that Morris's cynical approach made his skin crawl.[47]

It fell to the State Teacher Education, Certification, and Evaluation Committee to recommend "cutoff scores to the Department of Education." Susan May, who had signed the Central High letter in favor of testing, served on that committee. From the start, she says, Hillary, her walking partner, had been "shocked" about teacher competency. She really "showed her mettle," May says. Bill Clinton, she says, "showed his principles" and stood up to the threats. The debate in the Cutoff Committee about passing scores was angry and heated. It got "very personal and nasty," May says.[48] There were threats to her, and she was accused of racism and elitism. Despite May's protestations, the committee recommended 50 percent as a passing rate for reading and 60 percent as passing for math.

These recommendations were excoriated publicly; and, eventually, on a four-to-three vote on March 11, 1985, the cutoff passing rates for both reading and math were raised to 70 percent by the Board of Education.[49] Clinton praised the board for its brave decision. Today, he says he "tried not to get involved" with the debate over the cutoff scores, but he knew the scores had to be high enough "to pass the laugh test."[50]

The AEA would have none of it and conducted candlelight vigils and rallies against the test. It ultimately called on its membership to boycott the test. When the test was taken on March 23, 1985, less than 1,600 of the teacher force of 29,700 actually boycotted the test.[51]

Before the results were in, Bill Clinton was invited to appear with Peggy Nabors on the immensely popular *Phil Donahue*

Show, which was nationally televised, to debate teacher testing. Clinton had first said, "No," fearful that the program would open old wounds, and Representative Jodie Mahony had been ready to substitute. Then Clinton suddenly decided to do it.

Before a handpicked audience of 150 people (and an estimated national audience of 7 million), Clinton and Nabors made their points in a May 1, 1985, telecast in a highly charged atmosphere with Phil Donohue stoking the fire with pointed questions. Parents, teachers, and interested citizens added their comments. One parent argued that teacher testing would not fix our schools, while a grandparent represented the fact that teachers "would throw a wall-eyed fit if they have to take a test."[52] Civil rights attorney John Walker attacked the test as having racial undertones.[53]

Appearing on the *Phil Donahue Show* was the right decision for Clinton. He was reasonable in his explanations but forceful and passionate in defending the legislation. The nation had its first good look at Bill Clinton, and it liked what it saw.

Results of the teacher tests were published on June 26, 1985, and showed that 90 percent of the 28,276 teachers who took the test passed.[54] African American teachers did not do as well as whites, and that led to some racial bitterness. Accusations began to surface that the test discriminated against African Americans, but Clinton tactfully addressed the concerns on CBS's *Face the Nation* on July 7, 1985, saying:

> It appears, based on the geographic results, that the failure rate among black teachers was greater than the failure rate among white teachers. I agree that would be discriminatory if the test was given once and then if you didn't pass it you couldn't be recertified. . . . I believe the evidence is that black teachers can learn these skills and can do just as well as white teachers. And it may be that Arkansas is the first

> state in the country to prove that there is no difference based on race in God-given abilities and the ability to know and master. . . . Black children and the poor white children in our state . . . have no other shot but the public schools to have a decent education and a decent opportunity in life. We're doing this for them, and I reject the notion that it is discriminatory, and if after two years there's not a dramatic closing of whatever racial gap exists, I'll be the most surprised person in America.[55]

Later, in May of 1986, the AEA filed suit challenging the testing law on the basis of discrimination against black teachers. Clinton's reply was that an education committee, one-third of whom were black, evaluated the test positively on the basis of ability to do the job. The lawsuit was ultimately dismissed.

Bill Clinton, without question, did not have to tackle the issue of teacher testing. His advocacy for the other educational standards led to those standards being enacted into law. Surely he knew at the time that more went into being a good teacher than basic skills, like creativity in the classroom and the ability to relate to and inspire students to learn. He was appalled, though, by what Hillary had found on her tour of the state—that some teachers lacked basic literacy and math skills. Quite simply, he believed if that was the case, those teachers should not be in the classroom, and the people of the state agreed with him.

Arkansas teachers have forever been a strong political force, a fact never lost on a political animal like Bill Clinton. And the AEA had not endorsed Clinton in his comeback bid against Frank White in 1982. Its choice had first been Jim Guy Tucker until the runoff, when it gave its "lukewarm" endorsement to Clinton. Regardless of that, Clinton acted with considerable nerve and fortitude throughout the testing wars. Representative Charles R. Moore of Luxora summed up the feelings of many in the state when he heard the testing legislation had passed: "I have become

George Fisher shows Bill Clinton's commitment to education. *Published with permission of the* Arkansas Democrat-Gazette, *copyright September 18, 1983. Arkansas Arts Center Library Collection of George Fisher Cartoons.*

a great admirer of Mr. Clinton in the past few weeks. . . . [H]e's made some courageous decisions."[56]

Clinton now describes the teacher-testing legislation as a "seminal moment in Arkansas politics," and he is correct.[57] It certainly symbolized his education reform effort. Teacher testing was only done once in Arkansas, but its long-term impact was to bring additional focus to the *adequacy* of the education afforded in the classroom. This went hand-in-hand with the other standards proposed by Clinton and enacted at the 1983 special session. Almost twenty years later, adequacy would be the touchstone and barometer for constitutional compliance in the *Lake View* decision by the Arkansas Supreme Court.[58] That course was set in large part by what Clinton accomplished in 1983.

Jim Guy Tucker as governor. *David Pryor Papers, Special Collections, University of Arkansas Libraries, Fayetteville.*

Jim Guy Tucker
1992–1996

I am an idealist without illusions.

—JOHN F. KENNEDY

The event that Jim Guy Tucker had lived and prepared for his entire life was minutes away. At 4:45 p.m. on Monday, December 12, 1992, he was to be sworn in as the state's forty-third governor by Chief Justice Jack Holt Jr. in the chamber of the House of Representatives. President-elect Bill Clinton had just officially resigned as the state's chief executive. Under a recent Arkansas Supreme Court opinion, Tucker was eligible to be governor immediately after that resignation.

With quiet resolve and supreme confidence, Tucker repeated the oath after the chief justice carefully spoke the words. He then turned and kissed his wife, Betty, and pivoted toward Bill Clinton. They embraced in a bear hug. It was hugely emotional for both men—Clinton because he was leaving a job he dearly loved to face horrendous challenges and Tucker because of a dream now realized. They whispered mutual congratulatory words and separated for Tucker to make his inaugural address. He spoke of "great feelings" in Arkansas about the Clinton victory and the people's eagerness for Clinton's leadership.[1] Clinton was equally magnanimous in his remarks about Tucker and spoke of his competence and ability.

The reality, as is often the case, lay somewhere beneath the surface. Tucker and Clinton for decades had been the acknowledged golden boys of Arkansas politics. They had collided once in a fierce political battle when Clinton sought to reclaim the governor's seat from Frank White in 1982. Clinton had won the democratic primary, and Tucker had finished third. Tucker was now forty-nine, and Clinton, forty-six; and both showed signs of incipient grayness in their hair.

Though contemporaries with a shared devotion to politics and public policy, the two men were not close friends. Each begrudgingly respected the other, but like two bulls pawing the ground and knowing that conflict was inevitable, each had been highly suspicious of the other. A case in point was Jimmy Carter's campaign for president in 1976. Tucker, who was congressman for the state's second congressional district, was highly resentful of the fact that Clinton was selected by the Carter team to coordinate Arkansas for Carter. Tucker was given South Dakota. Tucker let the Carter people know he was displeased. Secretly, he knew Clinton would use the Carter campaign to build his own Arkansas organization which would present a future threat. Clinton did not appreciate Tucker's challenge.

Tucker eventually ran for lieutenant governor in 1990 and won. As Clinton sought his final term as Arkansas's governor, and because of Clinton's race for the presidency in 1992, Tucker, for much of that year, had been thrust into the role of acting governor. Not surprisingly, disputes arose between the peripatetic Clinton on the campaign trail and Tucker. Clinton's staff, who wanted to avoid any political embarrassment to Clinton in his bid for the presidency, sometimes presented obstacles to Tucker, who was tussling with the state's problems. At one point, Tucker fired Gloria Cabe, who was Clinton's chief of staff in the governor's office, which led to a sharp and frank exchange between the two men.[2]

But that was history, and now as the two men embarked on new journeys to meet their respectful challenges, there was, at least superficially, a feeling of well-being and goodwill. Yet, even in the middle of the celebration, there was one matter of immense concern for Tucker. The state's $1 billion Medicaid program, which provided health services for the poor, disabled, and elderly, affecting about 257,000 Arkansans, was in dire trouble. Medicaid, which had been expanded during the Clinton years for indigent pregnant women and small children, now had a $28 million shortfall and was hemorrhaging money at the rate of $3 million a week.[3] It needed an immediate and dramatic infusion of cash. Tax revenue would have to be generated in some form, and Clinton had given the problem to Tucker to resolve. The future of Medicaid was hanging in the balance. Ninety thousand Arkansans stood to lose their benefits in nineteen days.

Jim Guy Tucker's instincts have always been to fight. As he puts it, "it is part of my genes and training to attack."[4] Genetically, he came by it honestly. His paternal grandfather, Guy Tucker, had been marshal of Union County and was involved in a famous gun battle in October 1902 on the courthouse square in El Dorado. The Tucker-Parnell feud, as it was known, was legendary; and after the shooting, two of the Parnell brothers lay dead, and Guy Tucker was wounded.[5]

Jim Guy Tucker enjoyed football in his high school days and boxing at Harvard University. He joined the U.S. Marines and failed the physical to go to Vietnam due to an ulcerated colon, a condition that has plagued him his entire life. (In 1994, he almost died from gastrointestinal internal bleeding associated with a diseased liver.) He went to Vietnam anyway, but as a journalist, and wrote a book in 1968, *Arkansas Men at War,* dedicated to his future nemesis and aide to Senator J. William Fulbright, Jim McDougal.[6] While at law school at the University of Arkansas at Fayetteville, Tucker had a physical brawl with All-American football player Lloyd Phillips, though the reason for the brawl is somewhat murky. At one point, Tucker remembers being thrown across the hood of a car. A young woman intervened after several minutes and broke up the fight.[7]

The same instinct for combat and derring-do accompanied Tucker in his political campaigns, law practice, and business dealings. As prosecutor-elect for the Sixth Judicial District, he tried to enter Tucker Penitentiary undercover, Brubaker style, to investigate conditions. He was found out by prison officials and immediately removed. He would bring the same assertiveness to the job of governor. For the most part, it stood him in good stead in his legislative dealings. No one ever doubted in the state capitol where Jim Guy Tucker stood on an issue.

Says Richard Weiss, director of the Department of Finance and Administration, Tucker's approach to governance "was 180 degrees different from Clinton's." He could be "real abrupt and dictatorial" with agency heads and legislators. He was "meticulous and demanding . . . and could flat wear you out." After Bill Clinton, Weiss says, many in the legislature "welcomed someone telling them what do." But at times, says Weiss, Tucker "wouldn't take 'no' for an answer."[8]

Tucker's training had not only been to fight. Like Clinton before him, he was an incredibly quick study who devoured state data and could retain it and massage it. During his short term on the House Ways and Means Committee in Congress, some bills passing through the committee were said to be "Tuckerized" due to his intense analysis. Former gubernatorial aides, like Dent Gitchel, marveled at the fact that Tucker often knew the facts and had analyzed the issue of the moment much more in depth than his agency heads.[9] And with these same agency heads, Tucker could show his displeasure if they came unprepared. He did not suffer fools gladly.

As the newly installed governor, Tucker was now faced with the bankruptcy of the state's Medicaid program. The obvious fix was some new form of tax. But therein lay the problem. The estimate by Tucker was that $43 million was immediately needed in new revenue.[10] These funds could be generated by a sales tax on goods to be paid by all Arkansans or by special-interest taxes on items like tobacco, soft-drink syrups, luxury taxes, and certain legal and medical services. Advised by his financial team at the Department of Finance and Administration, which included Jim Pledger, Richard Weiss, and Tim Leathers, Tucker opted to tax the special interests. A tax package with these elements was cobbled together, and Tucker issued a call for a special session of the General Assembly on December 8, 1992.[11] It was as if war had been declared on the tobacco industry but, even more significantly, also on the soft-drink industry.

Those who remember the five-day special session in December 1992 describe it as a finely honed and orchestrated affair. Tucker had a business background, says former Representative Bobby Hogue of Jonesboro, and he could communicate with legislators who were mainly business people.[12] He was clearly in his honeymoon period and at the apex of his political power. He had political currency to spend, says former representative and now circuit judge Bynum Gibson.[13] Unlike Mike Huckabee, who would follow him in office, Tucker was intimately familiar with the legislative process and knew how to "work" the legislature. A stream of legislators filed down to his office during the session, or Tucker would run upstairs to the cloakrooms for each chamber and negotiate positions. It was battle, and Tucker was in his element.

In times of crisis, solutions will appear that have the beauty of simplicity. The cynical newspaper man H. L. Mencken once said, "There is always an easy solution to every problem—neat, plausible, and wrong."[14] So it was with the Medicaid crisis. The neat and plausible solution would be some increase in the sales tax. Tucker was convinced that would be wrong and that tobacco and soft drinks should be forced to pay to fix Medicaid. This would broaden the tax base as opposed to heaping an additional half-cent tax on the sale of goods on all Arkansans. Tucker did "what he thought was right," says Bobby Hogue today. "Once he made up his mind and told you something, you didn't have to look back."[15]

Armed with the strength of his convictions, Tucker advanced to sell his bailout plan of $163.5 million to be generated in the first full year of collection. Easily the most controversial part of the package was his five-cent excise tax per twelve ounces, which would be levied at the wholesale level on soft-drink ingredients such as syrup and powders. That was calculated to raise $7.7 million in fiscal 1993 and about $35.2 million the following fiscal year.[16] The soft-drink industry was outraged. Craig Rains, executive director of the Arkansas Soft Drink Association, said, "This was taking one small group and punishing them first because they like soft drinks."[17] Meanwhile, Representative Gus Wingfield of Delight offered his half-cent increase in the sales tax on all goods as an alternative, which was estimated to raise about $120 million a year.[18]

The day before the special session was to convene, Betty M. Brown, chair of the Coca-Cola Bottling Company of Northeast

Arkansas, announced plans to scrap a new $4.5 million bottling plant in Jonesboro if the soft-drink tax passed.[19] Tucker shot back and said that the soft-drink industry cared nothing for the sick and the elderly and was only being asked to pay its "fair share of the cost." He added, "The soft-drink lobbies don't really care whether old folks are kicked out of nursing homes in Arkansas or our education budget is savaged or our working people have to bear a heavier tax burden."[20]

On day one of the session, skepticism ran high as to the eventual passage of the tax. Part of the reason was the frenzied lobbying effort against the measure. As Tucker spoke to a group of elderly Arkansans supporting his plan in the capitol, soft-drink employees invaded the building rattling coins in soft drink cans. "Listen to the money rattling in their cans," Tucker said. "That is what they are interested in."[21] Meanwhile, the capitol building was surrounded by the soft-drink delivery trucks.

The second day of the session, a *Democrat-Gazette* headline read: "Soft-Drink Tax Fizzles." John Bland, a Royal Crown and Dr. Pepper bottler in Paragould, said Tucker's tax would "devastate" an industry.[22] The sponsor, Senator Steve Bell of Batesville, amended his bill to reduce the soft-drink tax to two cents per twelve ounces and to remove powders. Later, a two-cent tax passed the Senate, cutting estimated revenue to about $16 million in fiscal year 1994.[23]

The rawness of the lobbying effort against all of the taxes, but especially the soft-drink tax, was intense. Representative Earnest Cunningham of Helena said it was "the toughest he had had to face in 20 years."[24] Senator Stanley Russ of Conway said of Tucker, "He's putting his political career on the line" and "rubbing a lot of lobbyists the wrong way but he's doing it for a good reason."[25]

The final ploy to kill the soft-drink tax was the addition of chocolate to the elements to be taxed. Its sponsor, appropriately enough, was Representative "Sody" Arnold of Arkadelphia. On the last day of the session, Representative Ben McGee of Marion, who is said by Richard Weiss to be the man who originally floated the idea of taxing soft drinks, was successful with his allies in having chocolate removed from the bill.[26] Representative Jodie Mahony of El Dorado described the soft-drink lobby as the "laughingstock of the state" because of the chocolate amendment.[27]

Though the soft-drink tax was by far the most hotly debated aspect of Tucker's tax plan, his package, which included taxes on cigarettes, luxury services, home health care, and nursing services, ultimately passed; and the session, though it fell short of the target amount to be raised, was declared a success.

Bobby Hogue, who later would serve as Speaker of the House in the two regular sessions in 1993 and 1995, voted against the soft-drink tax. However, he questions his decision today. "It took a lot of guts to be able to do it [pass the tax]," he now says. The soft-drink industry was couching the tax as an attack on "the poor man's luxury."[28]

Tucker's management of the special session brought to the fore all of his political acumen as well as his intellect, assertiveness, tenacity, and hard work. It was a model of how to accomplish a legislative goal against fierce opposition from special interests. In a very real sense, it was Tucker's finest hour.

The end of Tucker's term as governor in 1996 is the stuff of tragedy. The tragic part is that he was caught up in the Whitewater investigation by special prosecutor Kenneth Starr. The focus, initially, had been on President Clinton, but it then extended to ensnare other peripheral figures like Tucker. He was charged with mail

George Fisher shows Jim Guy Tucker's Medicaid Christmas present. *Published with permission of the* Arkansas Democrat-Gazette, *copyright December 24, 1992. Arkansas Arts Center Library Collection of George Fisher Cartoons.*

fraud and conspiracy in federal court on August 17, 1995, tried for over three weeks, and ultimately convicted on May 28, 1996. If convicted, he had pledged he would resign as governor, effective July 15, 1996.

The denouement of the tragedy played out on that date—July 15, 1996. Shortly before Lieutenant Governor Mike Huckabee was to be sworn in at 2:00 p.m., Tucker reneged on his resignation in a telephone call to Huckabee and in a letter written to President Pro Tempore of the Senate Stanley Russ of Conway and Speaker of the House Bobby Hogue of Jonesboro.[29] His explanation was that a juror who sat on his convicting jury in federal court was tainted and biased against him due to his failure to commute the prison sentence of the husband of that juror. Based on this, he said he was stepping aside only for the lieutenant governor to assume the role of acting governor. Because of this temporary disability to serve out his term, he was placing his ultimate resignation on hold until the matter could be heard in federal court. He followed these letters with a press conference in the Governor's Conference Room. "If I am to resign, there should be a reason," he said. "The elimination of the verdict [the federal conviction] would eliminate the reason for my announced resignation."[30]

The hue and cry from the Huckabee supporters was immediate and shrill. Tucker, with his wife, Betty, by his side, was booed and cursed by those supporters as he made his way out of the state capitol and down to his car. He eventually would go to the Democratic State Party Headquarters and isolate himself. During the ensuing four hours, threats of impeachment were conveyed to Tucker by Hogue and Russ.[31] They advised him there was no support for his position in either chamber. Later that afternoon, Tucker wrote both men that he was resuming the full powers of the governorship to counter the threat of Huckabee's announced threat to call the legislature into session for purposes of Tucker's impeachment.

Then state Democratic Party chair Bynum Gibson is generally credited with bringing Tucker to his senses by a telephone call from his law office in Dermott. "Jim Guy Tucker was always going to do the right thing," Gibson says today.[32] But it was Gibson who helped direct him to that point by referring to the six o'clock news on television and to the fact that reversing his current stand and resigning immediately would ameliorate the situation and show the people of Arkansas that he was keeping his word. Gibson intimates that the threat of impeachment was not the way to get a fighter like Tucker to change his mind. Minutes later, Tucker followed Gibson's advice and resigned. The next day he would apologize to the people of Arkansas, saying what he had done was "wrong and inconsiderate," and he asked for Huckabee to accept his apology.[33]

Tucker's decision to rescind his resignation went beyond being merely misguided; it exhibited severely impaired judgment and served as testimony to the fact that his political prowess had been tremendously eroded by the rigors of his ill health, trial, conviction, and its aftermath. Falling from such heights and now suffering the daily torture of rejection, injustice, and humiliation, like some twentieth-century Prometheus, had taken its toll. His decision, nevertheless, threw the state of Arkansas into horrific chaos and was reminiscent, though nobody died, of the Brooks-Baxter War in 1874 over who would be the state's governor. State Democrats rued the moment, fearing fallout against them in future elections due to Tucker's partisan actions.

The bookends of Tucker's gubernatorial career stand out in stark relief. There is the brilliant political handling of the Medicaid crisis in December 1992 and his other successes in education, juvenile justice, and criminal procedure, followed by the disastrous resignation four years later. If his superb handling of the 1992 crisis and his legislative victory over entrenched special interests like the soft-drink industry define the man when healthy, surely the July 15, 1996, events are illustrative of a man, devastated and exhausted by events and a worsening liver condition, who had lost his political judgment.

It fell to the president of the Senate, Stanley Russ, to offer the most plausible explanation for what had occurred: "I felt I was seeing an impulsive response from a man who had been in combat for a year and was suffering from combat fatigue. He felt trapped. He was responding from a defensive position rather than from a controlled position, and it was all understandable to me."[34]

Mike Huckabee as governor. *Published with permission of the Ouachita Baptist University Special Library Collection.*

Mike Huckabee

1996–2007

No longer can the State operate on a "hands off" basis regarding how state money is spent in local school districts and what the effect of that spending is. Nor can the State continue to leave adequacy and equality considerations regarding school expenditures solely to local decision making.

—LAKE VIEW DECISION, NOVEMBER 21, 2002

The tsunami created by the Arkansas Supreme Court's *Lake View* decision on November 21, 2002, threatened a sea change in public education as it had been known, structured, and funded for decades.[1] The court's ruling struck down the formula used to fund public education on grounds that it fostered inequality in educational opportunity and offered students an inadequate product to boot. The court focused on abysmally low national rankings in per capita student expenditures; mediocre test scores; the substandard numbers of high school graduates, college graduates, and those with graduate-school degrees; graduates with an inability to read and write; inadequate teacher pay;

and abnormally high remediation requirements in college for English and math proficiency. The resulting mosaic evidenced an education system that was seriously broken and so dysfunctional that it jeopardized the future of the state.

Sixteen days before the *Lake View* decision was handed down, Mike Huckabee had been reelected to a new four-year term as governor. Because of Amendment 73 to the Arkansas Constitution, which limited the number of terms for constitutional officers, this would be his last term as governor. However, in less than two months, the General Assembly would meet in regular session to confront the education crisis fostered by the court decision. No one in state government knew quite what to do. Education funding already comprised fully one half of the state's budget with a total appropriation approaching $2 billion. If additional funds were required, where would the money come from? And for what new programs? The session had not yet begun and already the General Assembly's budgeting process had been derailed by the Arkansas Supreme Court and was in complete disarray.

It is not an exaggeration to say that a way of life—small town life in rural Arkansas—was perceived to be under attack by the court's *Lake View* ruling. School districts heretofore had always been governed by local school boards. Now the court had decided that public education was not to be controlled locally, but, to ensure equality and adequacy, it had to be not only funded in large part by the state but administered by the state as well. The dreaded fear of forced consolidation and annexation of school districts, which would eliminate small and substandard districts, loomed large, not to mention mandated school mergers in the Mississippi Delta, where some black schools lagged light years behind their white counterparts.

So it was that with grave doubts and not a little consternation the legislature met in joint session on January 14, 2003, to hear what newly reelected Governor Mike Huckabee had to say in his State of the State message. According to his eventual staunch ally on education matters, Senator Jim Argue of Little Rock, it was anybody's guess what Huckabee would do.[2] The smart money was betting that he would demonize the court and force a constitutional crisis by rejecting the court's ruling. That way, he could lionize local control of school districts, they speculated, and engage in rank demagoguery, George Wallace style. After all, when his predecessor, Jim Guy Tucker, had championed greater consolidation of school districts eight years earlier in an effort to better curriculum and administrative efficiency, Huckabee had piled on Tucker with certain legislative leaders and blasted his program as unworkable and naïve. Why would Huckabee change his position now?

Precisely at ten o'clock, the sergeant-at-arms announced the governor's presence to the House and Senate, and he entered with his ranking department heads, including director of education Ray Simon and selected representatives and senators escorting him. The air was tense, yet Huckabee appeared on his game. He strode down the center aisle toward the raised bench and podium, exuding an air of complete confidence and contentment, shaking hands warmly as he went. This was his fourth address to a joint session on his legislative proposals. He was seasoned now after seven years in office and comfortable in his role. The job and its challenges were no longer new to him. He arrived at the podium and turned around and reached for the hands of Lieutenant Governor Winthrop Paul Rockefeller and Speaker of the House Herschel Cleveland, who perched in their elevated seats as the leaders of the two legislative bodies. He then turned to the podium and began to speak.

Eschewing a prepared text on the teleprompter, he spoke in measured tones with a joke here, a quip there, and then segued into the regular clichés of "challenges to be met" and "opportunities to be reached." It was not until he turned to education that his words began to sing.

The history of public education in Arkansas has been known more for its failures than its successes. Before the Civil War, the estimate is that half the state's children were uneducated and illiterate.[3] Following the war, under a new state constitution and Union governor, public education took a foothold. But it was opposed by many in Arkansas who preferred to remain illiterate and not have educated children who would "turn against their parents." Anti-education feelings among whites were based on suspicion of northern Republicans, fear of educated blacks, concern over a debilitated workforce on the farm, and an alarm about the growing number of female teachers in a profession that needed to be male dominated.

In the 1920s, there were thousands of isolated school districts in Arkansas cut off by dismal road conditions, particularly in the hills of northwestern Arkansas. Roads throughout the state gradually improved during that decade, and better roads meant better schools. Such was the slogan of Governor John M. Martineau in 1926. But still, at the end of the '20s, a systematic study of education in Arkansas concluded: "For thousands upon thousands of children, Arkansas is providing absolutely no chance. To these children, to be born in Arkansas is a misfortune and an injustice from which they will never recover, and upon which they will look back with bitterness when plunged into adult life, into competition with students born in other states which today are providing more liberally for their children."[4] The dearth of high schools in the state was proof positive of the disaster. Forty-two percent of white children had no approved high school to attend, and for blacks it was worse.

In 1948, under Initiated Act No. 1, which the people passed overwhelmingly, progress was made due to forced consolidation and annexation of small school districts (fewer than 350 students), which reduced the number of districts from 1,589 to 421. But an Arkansas Supreme Court decision limited the application of this act; and, thereafter, forced consolidation based on the 350-students limit fell into disuse.

The saga of education reform in Arkansas for the past fifty years has been a rambling, rambunctious tale filled occasionally with sound and fury but more often than not with much posturing and paralyzing inertia. The story of "The Emperor's New Clothes" comes to mind. Something was dreadfully wrong in education, and most observers knew what it was, but few had the political will to come to grips with it.

Despite Arkansas's questionable commitment to education over its history, most Arkansans believed that better education was a good thing for the state. It led to industry, economic development, and jobs. It was said that mothers in particular wanted something more for their children and knew beyond peradventure that education was the gateway for their success. But standing as a formidable impediment to that dream of something better was the perceived sacrifice of an entrenched way of life to get there. Rural Arkansas was rooted in small-town life which had as an essential component its schools. Take away our schools by the merger or consolidation of our school districts and you take away our identity was the common complaint. Then there were the costs associated with transportation to another school district and the myriad fears that surrounded social readjustment in a neighboring school. And would local superintendents with iron-fisted control over their districts, and in some instances control over hiring-and-firing decisions and who would start on the football team, willingly give up that authority?

There was, too, race, which was the largely unspoken issue in much of the school-district-consolidation debate. Would non-performing minority schools be foisted upon their nearby white neighbors, thereby causing healthy schools to be dragged down in the process? The issues were complex, and reactions to all these issues were visceral and painful to ponder.

Hence, not much had been done to address root-and-branch problems in education since the state's inception. Band-aid solutions had been the order of the day for the last fifty years, with tinkering here, spot funding there. An Arkansas Supreme Court decision had addressed the inequality of per-pupil funding in 1983 (*Dupree v. Alma School District*), which Bill Clinton addressed with the sales-tax increase, curriculum and assessment standards, and teacher testing in the special session in 1983.[5] But whether the education afforded to Arkansas students was *adequate* so as to enable Arkansas's students to compete and function in the emerging global community had largely been left unexamined on a wholesale basis until the *Lake View* decision in 2002.

Mike Huckabee had always been an anomaly. The first member of his family to graduate from high school, he then graduated from college, Ouachita Baptist University, and became a Baptist minister who ultimately made the transition to politician and governor. In the process, he had been lucky. In 1993, he defeated the Democratic Party's nominee for lieutenant governor, Nate Coulter, in a race that Coulter should have easily won. Evangelical and Baptist support for Huckabee was part of the reason for his win, but a wan and pale Coulter speaking in his ads in contrast to an energetic and vibrant Huckabee also played a role in his defeat. Then, Governor Jim Guy Tucker resigned from office July 15, 1996, due to a felony conviction for fraudulent transactions, and Huckabee was sworn in as governor. His Democratic opponents in the aftermath in 1998 and 2002 were not up to the task of removing the popular governor, though his margin of victory over democratic contender Jimmie Lou Fisher in 2002 had dwindled to 53 percent.

By and large, Arkansans were comfortable with Mike Huckabee. He was real, and he was one of them. He liked bass fishing and hunting. He played bass guitar in his band (Capitol Offense), and he had a sense of humor, which, while sometimes tending to the scatological, usually was hilarious. He had weight problems which he tackled with vigor by long-distance running and a medical diet. He also wrote a book about it all, *Quit Digging Your Grave with a Knife and Fork.*[6] While the mansion was being renovated in 2000, he moved into a triple-wide trailer on the mansion grounds, drawing national attention and solidifying the redneck vote.

His public persona aside, Huckabee was a complex man. Intelligent, glib, devout, he also could be thin skinned and was known for a vindictive streak, especially in his early years in politics. On occasion, he wore a pronounced chip on his shoulder, which gave way to biting sarcasm. He was also easy prey for prisoners who announced their religious conversions, asked for forgiveness, and petitioned for clemency. While some of his reduced sentences may well have been successful, others had horrendous consequences. Maurice Clemmons, following parole, murdered four police officers in Seattle, Washington, in November 2009. Also, Wayne Dumond, after his parole while Huckabee was governor, was convicted of rape and murder in 2003 in Missouri.

Huckabee also did not pull punches in his political campaigns. A major campaign issue against Dale Bumpers in the 1992 race for the U.S. Senate largely centered on Bumpers's support for one artist (Robert Mapplethorpe) whom Huckabee dubbed as pornographic. The issue morphed into an accusation that Bumpers supported the use of taxpayer money for pornographic displays. While Mapplethorpe's art could not be termed mainstream in any sense, the issue was sensational and lacked substance. Bumpers won the election easily with 60 percent of the votes.

"Now let me mention a second important issue that faces us here," Huckabee continued to the legislature in a voice that was strained and rose slightly in volume. "I think you expect it—the restructuring of education. Just a few days after the elections, the Supreme Court handed down a sweeping decision in the Lake View case. It's not enough for us to try and improve education. We must triumph in this effort. The courts have ordered it."[7]

He continued on and, focusing on his note cards, began to make his case for a complete education overhaul premised on the failures of the past. Unbeknownst to the legislature, his friend and then U.S. attorney Bud Cummins had given him a book on past State of the State addresses. Huckabee proceeded to quote seven past governors—Tom McRae, Marion Futrell, Homer Adkins, Francis Cherry, Winthrop Rockefeller, Dale Bumpers, and Bill Clinton—all of whom had sounded the clarion call for improved education in their speeches. And, still, only "minor adjustments" to a broken system had been made, he said. Not too subtly, he chastised his predecessors for talking a good game but, when it got down to cases, "not walking the walk."

He then issued a bold challenge: "Ladies and gentlemen of

this 84th General Assembly, I ask you to join me in not being another footnote in the pages of Arkansas history, where we merely come and give lip service to how much we have improved something that will only land us right back in the courts. And we'll continue to lose until we finally stand up, step up and do what we must in this session do for our children. And that is fulfill the constitutional mandate for an adequate, efficient, suitable, equitable education for every single boy and girl in this state. I ask you to join me in the courage for that task."[8]

He concluded: "This is not a fight I led us into, but it's one I'm willing and prepared to lead us through with your help and with God's. Let's be clear in understanding we cannot always do what we like or even what we agree with. But the real test of leadership is being able to lead not only in the battles that we choose but also in the battles that choose us. To do what we're required to do to meet the needs of our students and the demands of the court order, we have to be willing, if necessary, to sacrifice our political lives for the sake of our children's future in order that we would fulfill our obligations that we swore under oath that we would fulfill."[9]

He then fleshed out the centerpiece of his proposal, which was to reduce the 310 existing school districts in the state to 130 with a kindergarten through twelfth-grade enrollment of 1,500 total students or more in each remaining school district.

Huckabee would later say that he watched the legislators' "jaws drop on their desks" when he made his speech.[10] Rex Nelson, a communication aide to the governor at the time, said the speech had been a Manhattan Project as far as secrecy. Huckabee "loves to shock," Nelson says.[11] Whatever the case, the legislature was astonished by his embrace of the consolidation issue.

When the address ended, Senator Jim Argue stood in awe.

He admitted later that, simply put, Huckabee was a "better man" than he had thought. Huckabee's decision to support the court's decision in *Lake View* and go even further was one "of conscience," Argue said.[12] Over the ensuing months, Huckabee never wavered in his support for a reorganization of school districts so that a floor student population of 1,500 students could be reached rather than the 350 students that ultimately resulted.

It is true that in 2003 Governor Mike Huckabee knew he could not run for another term as governor due to Amendment 73 to the Arkansas Constitution, limiting the number of terms he could serve to two. Thus, the potential political ramifications from his consolidation speech might be minimized. And yet a race for the U.S. Senate was certainly a distinct possibility, as well as a race for the presidency. He ultimately decided on the latter race, where he lost the Republican nomination for president to Arizona senator John McCain in 2008.

Why did Huckabee reverse his position and fight so zealously for school consolidation and better standards from 2003 forward? He says that, though it sounds "smaltzy" and as if he had "just come down from Walton Mountain," it was a "principled decision and the right thing to do." He wanted to make a difference in education, he says. He told his staff, "We need to do the best we can regardless of the consequences."[13]

But the more practical explanation was economic. Without consolidation and the larger student body of 1,500 students, the cost per student to offer the same courses necessary for an *adequate* education for smaller schools would be prohibitive. Having a larger pool of students to service was simply an "economies of scale" issue, he says. He credits Education Director Ray Simon with developing the consolidation plan. "Simon was the chemist," Huckabee says, "and I was the pharmacist."[14]

The high number of college students in remediation courses was also proving too costly. To develop basic skills in English and mathematics was surely a driving force. On this point, Huckabee says, "We found ourselves paying college costs" in reference to remediation courses in college "for a high school education."[15]

Through all the controversy, which he attributes in large part to the recalcitrance of the superintendents who went "crazy" when they heard his speech, he "focused on the light," he says, which was what he and his team were trying to accomplish, "and not the heat," which was the argument from opposing forces. He says today that his core group was made up of Senator Argue and Ray Simon, but also two African American legislators, Representatives Calvin Johnson of Pine Bluff and Robert White of Camden, who, he says, were stalwarts. This was the "notorious partnership," he says.[16] A third African American representative, Joyce Elliot, also proved to be effective in her support, says Jim Argue.[17]

During the *Lake View* wars that were waged over the next four years, Huckabee says he was constantly amazed by legislators and other political leaders who told him, "You're right," but who would not come out publicly and support him. He also was disappointed that the Arkansas Supreme Court never required consolidation of the schools in the *Lake View* decisions because that would have given him "cover," he adds.[18]

"We had to settle for much less than 1,500 students per school district," he says with some dismay. "The ultimate figure was 350, and we settled for too little. The number was whittled down by compromises and tinkering. At one point, we thought we had a deal with the superintendents for 750 students, but that deal fell apart in three hours."[19]

And yet, with all the frustration associated with setting a high bar and failing to cross it, he admits he is proud of what was

Photograph of initial supporters of Mike Huckabee's consolidation bill in January 2003, including representatives of the AEA and Chamber of Commerce but also the "notorious partnership," as Huckabee dubbed it: Representative Robert White of Camden (*far left*), Senator Jim Argue (*second from the left*), and Representative Calvin Johnson of Pine Bluff (*fourth from the left*)." *From the private collection of Jim Argue and published with his permission.*

achieved for the first time—a minimum number of 350 students, kindergarten through twelfth grade, for each school district was written into law in 2003.[20] Schools were also made more accountable in the sense that with students' success came increased funding. He has no doubt that student populations will continue to grow in each school district in order to meet the standards. Plus, he has watched as the standards and the full panoply of mandated programs gradually reduce the number of school districts, where today that number is 244 and steadily dropping.[21]

Mike Huckabee's moment in history was to challenge a strongly entrenched cultural phenomenon in the form of small-town Arkansas in an effort to make Arkansas and its children

George Fisher cartoon on consolidation and local school districts, published earlier than 2003 but depicting the fierce opposition of local communities. *Published with permission of the* Arkansas Democrat-Gazette, *copyright March 28, 1983. Arkansas Arts Center Library Collection of George Fisher Cartoons.*

better. When he did it so vigorously, he placed his political career and even his personal safety in jeopardy. Rex Nelson recalls that in some cases, Huckabee's security detail had to be doubled because feelings ran so deep against him at town meetings.[22] A meeting in Stuttgart comes particularly to Nelson's mind. In other instances, he was simply not invited to political events due to the animosity he engendered over the consolidation issue.

Huckabee's answer to the furor is best illustrated by his Wal-Mart analogy. He made the argument to rural communities that you drive thirty miles to Wal-Mart to shop for better merchandise and a wider selection. Why not do the same for your children and their education? They would answer invariably, he says, "That's not the same thing." But Huckabee was convinced it was.[23]

It was a "historical" speech, Ray Simon says today, referring back to the 2003 State of the State address which he, no doubt, played a large part in drafting. It was meant to reorganize and reduce the school districts in the state, he adds, not the number of schools, but the number of school districts. Plus, "sound research" had identified 1,500 students as the target size for a kindergarten-through-twelfth-grade efficient school district to operate. That size would render an economically efficient school system with a core group of students to be offered a "rigorous curriculum" and for other standards to be met. But even so, "1,500 was not a drop-dead figure," he says; we were "flexible" on that, if you could prove you could meet the standards with fewer students in the district.[24]

The foundation for consolidation had been laid in 1998 with the Smart Start and Smart Step programs,[25] which set curriculum standards and goals in reading and math, says Simon, and also provided economic incentives to the schools as well as remediation plans to provide additional help to students. The reduced number of school districts now "is all due to Mike Huckabee," he says. He concludes, "Buddy, I tell you. Arkansas is a player now."[26]

Simon, in his enthusiasm, overstates Huckabee's role. Other governors like Clinton and Tucker had toiled long and hard in the education vineyards to improve standards and to foster an adequate education in Arkansas. And the Arkansas General Assembly, in the wake of the *Lake View* decisions, enacted breathtaking legislation for the Arkansas schools.

What cannot be gainsaid, however, is that Huckabee seized the moment presented to him by the *Lake View* decision in 2003 and fought long and hard for the most controversial aspect of public school reform—consolidation and annexation of school districts, which were not included in the 2002 decision. The personal opposition to him could not have been more rancorous. Some legislators, like Senator Jim Jeffress of Crossett, would intimate, according to Huckabee, that if consolidation passed, honeydew melons would lose their fragrance and the fish would stop biting. The demagoguery and exploitation of the issue was "disgusting," he says. He knew, he adds, that without reorganization of school districts, an adequate education based on an enhanced curriculum would not become a reality for those students most in need.[27] Without Huckabee's tenacity and leadership, what he accomplished in school reform, though not his total dream, would not have come to fruition. He did it, Ray Simon says, because of "his personal care for children. He has a special place in his heart for children."[28]

EPILOGUE

If there is a constant thread that weaves throughout this book, it is that our governors fill a critical role for our state that oftentimes requires extraordinarily difficult decisions to be made. For the most part, our governors over the past sixty plus years have responded courageously. My intent has been to show how supremely difficult the job can be and to hold up for examination important snapshots in the careers of these men that exhibit and reveal their personal character.

Arkansas has been blessed with a wide array of talented chief executives. All of the governors profiled in this book fall into that category. The job, however, eventually takes the measure of its officeholders, and this book has examined instances where that has been the case.

One unassailable conclusion is that effectiveness requires not only courage but an abundance of what Arkansas Supreme Court Justice George Rose Smith used to call "just plain horse sense." The two must go hand in hand for one to confront a significant crisis with some measure of success. The subjects of this book had their moments of truth. How they dealt with those moments gives us a historical roadmap and insight into some of Arkansas's most dynamic political figures.

INTERVIEWS

Jim Argue, former state senator from Little Rock, July 16, 2009, Little Rock, AR

Mike Beebe, governor of Arkansas, July 24, 2009, Little Rock, AR

Sam Bratton, former legislative assistant to Governor Bill Clinton, August 18, 2009, Little Rock, AR

Dale Bumpers, former governor of Arkansas and former U.S. senator, August 15, 2009, Little Rock, AR

Marion Burton, former aide to Governor Winthrop Rockefeller, July 21, 2009, Little Rock, AR

Preston Bynum, executive secretary for Governor Frank White, August 5, 2009, Little Rock, AR

Bill Clinton, former governor of Arkansas and former president of the United States, telephone interview, December 13, 2009

Ernie Dumas, columnist for *Arkansas Times,* May 14, 2009, Little Rock, AR

G. Thomas Eisele, former aide to Governor Winthrop Rockefeller and now U.S. Federal District judge, July 21, 2009, Little Rock, AR

Bynum Gibson, former state representative and current circuit judge, telephone interview, November 16, 2009

Dent Gitchel, former staff assistant for Governor Jim Guy Tucker and law professor, November 17, 2009, Little Rock, AR

Henry Hodges, former state representative, September 16, 2009, Little Rock, AR

Bobby Hogue, former Speaker of the House of Representatives, November 16, 2009, Little Rock, AR

Cliff Hoofman, former state representative and senator and now member of the Arkansas Highway Commission, telephone interview, September 2009

Mike Huckabee, former governor of Arkansas, September 29, 2009, North Little Rock, AR

Carl Hunt, telephone interview, February 15, 2010

Jim Johnson, former justice of the Arkansas Supreme Court and political candidate against Orval Faubus, Winthrop Rockefeller, and J. William Fulbright, telephone interview, November 14, 2009

Tim Leathers, deputy director of Arkansas Department of Finance and Administration, November 17, 2009, Little Rock, AR

Jodie Mahony, former state representative and senator from El Dorado, August 10, 2009, Little Rock, AR

David Malone, former state representative and senator, telephone interview, November 10, 2009

Susan May, former teacher at Central High School, telephone interview, November 25, 2009

Phil McMath, son of Governor Sid McMath, August 12, 2009, Little Rock, AR

Peggy Nabors, former president of the Arkansas Education Association, November 17, 2009, Little Rock, AR

Rex Nelson, columnist and former staff assistant to Governor Mike Huckabee, October 13, 2009, Little Rock, AR

David Pryor, former governor of Arkansas and former U.S. senator, September 22, 2009, Little Rock, AR

Bill Simmons, political editor for the *Arkansas Democrat-Gazette,* July 9, 2009, Little Rock, AR

Ray Simon, former director of Arkansas Department of Education, telephone interview, October 20, 2009

Robert D. Smith III, political affairs consultant, August 6, 2009, Little Rock, AR

Scott Stafford, former staff assistant for Governor Jim Guy Tucker and University of Arkansas at Little Rock law professor, November 9, 2009, Little Rock, AR

Alex Streett, former prosecuting attorney from Russellville, telephone interview, October 13, 2009

Jim Guy Tucker, former governor of Arkansas, November 10, 2009, Little Rock, AR

Joan Vehik, former bill clerk for numerous governors, including Governor Frank White, and staff assistant to Governor David Pryor, July 23, 2009, Little Rock, AR

John Ward, former aide to and biographer of Governor Winthrop Rockefeller, July 21, 2009, Little Rock, AR

Richard Weiss, director of Arkansas Department of Finance and Administration, November 17, 2009, Little Rock, AR

Gay White, widow of Governor Frank White, October 19, 2009, Little Rock, AR

NOTES

Sid McMath

1. David McCullough, *Truman* (New York: Simon & Schuster, 1992), 586.
2. Ibid.
3. Ibid., 587.
4. Sidney S. McMath, *Promises Kept* (Fayetteville: University of Arkansas Press, 2003), 196.
5. Ibid.
6. Ibid., 21.
7. Ibid., 22.
8. Ibid., 24.
9. Ibid., 6.
10. Phillip McMath, interview with author, August 12, 2009, Little Rock, AR.
11. McMath, *Promises Kept,* xxv.
12. Anne Phillips McMath in 1947 eventually shot and killed McMath's father, Hal McMath, in an act of self-defense. McMath, *Promises Kept,* 190.
13. McMath, *Promises Kept,* 195.
14. Ibid., 199.
15. Ibid., 202.
16. Ibid., 203.
17. *Arkansas Gazette,* September 24, 1948, 1.
18. Ibid.
19. Ibid., September 25, 1948, 1.
20. Ibid., October 9, 1948, 1.
21. Ibid., October 26,1948, 1.
22. Ibid., November 5, 1948, 1.
23. Ibid., September 30, 1957, 1.
24. McMath, *Promises Kept,* 207.

Francis Cherry

1. Michael B. Dougan, *Encyclopedia of Arkansas History and Culture* (Little Rock: Butler Center for Arkansas Studies, 2009), Francis Cherry, 2.
2. Amendment 42 to the Arkansas Constitution (approved November 4, 1952).
3. Roy Reed, *Faubus* (Fayetteville: University of Arkansas Press, 1997), 87.
4. Ibid., 92.
5. Ibid.
6. Ibid., 96.

7. Orval Faubus, *Down from the Hills* (Little Rock: Pioneer Press, 1980), 36.
8. Reed, *Faubus,* 93.
9. Faubus, *Down from the Hills,* 39.
10. Ibid., 40.
11. Ibid., 45.
12. Reed, *Faubus,* 88–91.
13. Ibid., 88.
14. Ibid., 124.

Orval Faubus

1. Elizabeth Jacoway, *Turn Away Thy Son* (New York: Free Press, 2007), 119.
2. Harry Ashmore, *Arkansas Gazette,* "A Time of Testing," September 1, 1957.
3. Orval Faubus, *Down from the Hills* (Little Rock: Pioneer Press, 1980), 197–208.
4. Roy Reed, *Faubus* (Fayetteville: University of Arkansas Press, 1997), 65.
5. Ibid., 106, 107.
6. Ibid., 84.
7. Ibid., 60.
8. Ibid., 131.
9. Ibid., 157.
10. Ibid., 163.
11. See Jacoway, *Turn Away,* 34.
12. Faubus, quoted in Reed, *Faubus,* 181.
13. Arkansas Constitution, Amend. 44, section 1 (approved November 6, 1956). See Kay Collett Goss, *The Arkansas State Constitution, A Reference Guide* (Westport, CT: Greenwood Press, 1983). Amendment 44 was repealed by a vote of the people in 1990.
14. Act 83 of 1957, Acts of Arkansas.
15. Act 84 of 1957, Acts of Arkansas.
16. Act 85 of 1957, Acts of Arkansas.
17. Reed, *Faubus,* 192.
18. Ibid., 190.
19. Jacoway, *Turn Away,* 117.
20. Ibid., 203.
21. Reed, *Faubus,* 200.
22. Ibid., 200.
23. Jim Johnson, telephone interview with author, November 14, 2009. Johnson died on February 14, 2010.
24. Ibid.
25. Reed, *Faubus,* 193.
26. Johnson, telephone interview with author.
27. Ibid.
28. Letter from Jim Johnson to author, dated November 16, 2009.
29. Johnson, telephone interview with author.

30. Ibid.

31. Faubus, *Down from the Hills*, 197, 207.

32. Ibid., 198.

33. Faubus, quoted in David Pryor, *A Pryor Commitment* (Little Rock: Butler Center Books, 2008), 218.

34. Harry Ashmore, *Civil Rights and Wrongs* (New York: Pantheon Books, 1994), 313.

WINTHROP ROCKEFELLER

1. *Arkansas Gazette*, April 5, 1968, 2A.

2. Ibid., April 7, 1968, 1A, 16A.

3. Ibid., April 6, 1968, 2.

4. *Arkansas Democrat*, April 7, 1968, 14A; *Arkansas Gazette*, April 6, 1968, 2.

5. *Arkansas Gazette*, April 6, 1968, 2.

6. Ibid., April 7, 1968, 1A.

7. John Ward, *The Arkansas Rockefeller* (Baton Rouge: Louisiana State University Press, 1978), 2 and following.

8. Cathy Irwin, *Agenda for Reform* (Fayetteville: University of Arkansas Press, 1991), 11.

9. Ibid., 20.

10. Ibid., 19.

11. Ibid., 20.

12. Ibid.

13. Ibid., 51.

14. Ibid., 55.

15. Ibid., 56.

16. Ward, *Rockefeller*, 60.

17. Ibid.,

18. Irwin, *Agenda*, p. 139.

19. Ibid., 188.

20. Act 362 of 1967, Acts of Arkansas.

21. *Arkansas Gazette*, April 8, 1968, 1A.

22. Ibid.

23. Ward, *Rockefeller*, 166.

24. *Arkansas Gazette*, April 8, 1968, 1A.

25. Ward, *Rockefeller*, 166.

26. Ibid., 162, 176.

27. Ibid., 176.

28. Judge Thomas Eisele, John Ward, Marion Burton, joint interview with author, July 21, 2009, Little Rock, AR.

Dale Bumpers

1. The author attended the 1973 legislative meetings and recounts this scene from memory.

2. Marlin Hawkins, *How I Stole Elections* (self-published, 1991).

3. Dale Bumpers, interview with author, August 15, 2009, Little Rock, AR. Bumpers's panel discussion as part of Kumpuris Lecture Series, Clinton Presidential Library, March 24, 2009.

4. Hawkins, *Elections,* 318; *Arkansas Gazette,* March 16, 1973, 1A.

5. Dale Bumpers, *Best Lawyer in a One Lawyer Town* (New York: Random House, 2003), 74–80.

6. An example of Bumpers's recount of the Roosevelt story was at the banquet for retired Arkansas Supreme Court justices at the governor's mansion, where he was the guest speaker, September 24, 2009. The author retells the story in his own words.

7. For entire text of Bumpers's impeachment speech, see Bumpers, *Best Lawyer,* 277–293.

8. Mary Lefkovitz, "Classic Oratory," *New York Times,* January 24, 1999, sec. 4, 15.

9. Alex Streett, telephone interview with author, October 13, 2009.

10. Ibid.

11. Bumpers, *Best Lawyer,* 165–169.

12. *Arkansas Legislative Digest,* Veto Message, February 6, 1973.

13. Bumpers, interview with author.

14. Ibid. Author retells story in his own words.

15. *Arkansas Gazette,* March 7, 1973, p. 1A

16. *Arkansas Gazette,* March 16, 1973, 2A. All quotations from Sparks in this paragraph are from this article.

17. *Arkansas Gazette,* March 16, 1973, 2A.

18. Bumpers, *Best Lawyer,* 226. Story also recounted in Bumpers's speech, September 24, 2009.

19. Bumpers's speech, September 24, 2009.

20. Truman, quoted in Bumpers, *Best Lawyer,* 226.

21. Bumpers, Kumpuris Lecture Series, Clinton Presidential Library.

David Pryor

1. Flood Control Act of 1938, Public Law No. 75–701

2. A sample of George Fisher's "Keep Busy" cartoons is included as an illustration in this book.

3. Neil Compton, *The Battle for the Buffalo River* (Fayetteville: University of Arkansas Press, 1992), 243–246.

4. David Pryor, speech to Arkansas Historical Association, Southern Arkansas University, April 25, 2009.

5. Pryor, speech to Historical Association.

6. David Pryor, *A Pryor Commitment* (Little Rock: Butler Center Books, 2008), 240.

7. Ibid., 20–25.

8. Ibid., 215.

9. Ibid., 216.

10. Ibid., 218; Orval Faubus, *Down from the Hills,* 205. Leggett was later executed in 1960.

11. David Pryor, introduction of Dale Bumpers, retired Arkansas Supreme Court justices' banquet, September 24, 2009.

12. Pryor, *Commitment,* 218.

13. Ibid.

14. Pryor, speech to Historical Association; Pryor, *Commitment,* 238.

15. Pryor, *Commitment,* 238.

16. Ibid., 237.

17. Lester Clayton, quoted in *Arkansas Gazette,* August 31, 1975, 5A.

18. *Arkansas Gazette,* August 31, 1975, 5A.

19. Earl T. Peebles, quoted in *Arkansas Gazette,* March 21, 1975, 1B.

20. *Arkansas Gazette,* July 10, 1975, 1A–3A. Letter quoted in following paragraphs.

21. Mrs. Robie Hash, quoted in *Arkansas Gazette,* August 31, 1975, 5A.

22. Pryor, speech to Historical Association.

23. *Arkansas Gazette,* July 20, 1975, 3E.

24. Ibid., August 31, 1975, 1A.

25. Associated Press, July 10, 1975.

26. *Arkansas Gazette,* Editorial, August 28, 1976, 4A.

27. *Arkansas Gazette,* January 18, 1977, 1B.

28. Ibid.

29. Ibid., January 26, 1977, 1B; February 1, 1977, 5A.

30. Ibid., February 4, 1977, 1B.

31. David Pryor, interview with author, September 22, 2009, Little Rock, AR.

32. Pryor, speech to Historical Association.

Frank White

1. Robert L. Brown, "Arkansas 'Gruff Gus' in the Governor's Seat," *Arkansas Times* (June 1981): 65.

2. Ibid.

3. Ibid., 64.

4. Gay White, interview with author, October 19, 2009, Little Rock, AR.

5. Carl Hunt, telephone interview with author, February 15, 2010.

6. Brown, "Arkansas 'Gruff Gus,'" 63.

7. Ibid., 66–67.

8. Ibid.

9. Preston Bynum, interview with author, August 5, 2009, Little Rock, AR.

10. Bill Clinton, *My Life* (New York: Alfred A. Knopf 2004), 280–281.

11. *Epperson v. Arkansas,* 393 U.S. 97 (U.S. Supreme Court, November 12, 1968).
12. *State v. Epperson,* 242 Ark. 922, 416 S.W. 2d 332 (Arkansas Supreme Court, July 26, 1967).
13. Act 590 of 1921, Acts of Arkansas.
14. *Arkansas Gazette,* March 20, 1981, p. 1A.
15. Ibid., 2A,
16. Ibid., 1A.
17. Ibid., 4A.
18. Cliff Hoofman, telephone interview with author, September 2009.
19. Ibid.
20. *Arkansas Gazette,* March 27, 1981, 3A.
21. Ibid.
22. *McLean v. Arkansas Board of Education,* 529 F. Supp. 1255 (Federal District Court for the Eastern District of Arkansas, January 5, 1982).
23. *Edwards v. Aguillard,* 482 U.S. 578 (U.S. Supreme Court, June 19, 1987).
24. Ernie Dumas, interview with author, May 14, 2009, Little Rock, AR.
25. Bynum, interview with author; Gay White, interview with author, October 19, 2009, Little Rock, AR.
26. Gay White, interview with author.
27. Ibid. Frank White died on May 21, 2003.

Bill Clinton

1. Though the depiction of this scene springs from the imagination of the author, many of Bill Clinton's thoughts were conveyed to the author in a telephone interview on December 13, 2009.
2. Bill Clinton, *My Life* (New York: Alfred A. Knopf, 2004), 308.
3. Hillary Rodham Clinton, *Living History* (New York: Simon & Schuster, 2003), 93.
4. *Dupree v. Alma School District No. 30,* 279 Ark. 340, 651 S. W. 2d 90 (Arkansas Supreme Court, May 31, 1983).
5. B. Clinton interview.
6. H. Clinton, *Living History,* 94.
7. B. Clinton, *My Life,* 309.
8. Ibid.
9. B. Clinton interview.
10. Letter from approximately seventy Central High School teachers to Governor Bill Clinton, dated September 21, 1983 (private records of Elaine Dumas).
11. *Arkansas Gazette,* November 20, 1983; January 28, 1984; April 1, 1985; B. Clinton, *My Life,* 310.
12. B. Clinton interview
13. Sam Bratton, interview with author, August 18, 2009, Little Rock, AR.
14. Proclamation, Acts of Arkansas, 1983 Extraordinary Session, 1272.
15. Peggy Nabors, interview with author, November 17, 2009, Little Rock, AR.
16. Ibid.

17. Ibid.
18. David Malone, telephone interview with author, November 10, 2009.
19. *Arkansas Gazette,* October 19, 1983, 1A.
20. Ibid., October 20, 1983, 8A.
21. B. Clinton interview.
22. Cliff Hoofman, telephone interview with author, September 2005.
23. Ermalee Boice, quoted in *Arkansas Gazette,* October 27, 1983, 20A.
24. H. Clinton, *Living History,* 95.
25. *Arkansas Gazette,* October 28, 1983, 8A.
26. B. Clinton, *My Life,* 311.
27. Bratton interview.
28. Jodie Mahony, interview with author, August 10, 2009, Little Rock, AR.
29. B. Clinton interview.
30. *Arkansas Gazette,* October 29, 1983, 1A; B. Clinton, *My Life,* 311.
31. *Arkansas Gazette,* October 28, 1983, 1A.
32. John Lisle, quoted in *Arkansas Gazette,* November 2, 1983, 3A.
33. Terry Humble, quoted in *Arkansas Gazette,* November 2, 1983, opinion page.
34. Bill Clinton, quoted in *Arkansas Gazette,* November 8, 1983, 4A.
35. Ermalee Boice, quoted in *Arkansas Gazette,* November 18, 1983, 1A.
36. Bill Clinton, quoted in *Arkansas Gazette,* November 18, 1983, 8A.
37. Ibid., November 20, 1983, 4A.
38. Ibid., January 25, 1984, 1B.
39. *Arkansas Gazette,* January 28, 1984, 7A.
40. Bill Clinton, quoted in *Arkansas Gazette,* March 31, 1984, 8A.
41. *Arkansas Gazette,* November 21, 1984.
42. Ibid., February 26, 1985, 8A.
43. Robert L. Kennedy, "Arkansas Teacher Testing: A Penny for Your Scores," paper presented at the Annual Meeting of the American Evaluation Association, Boston, Massachusetts, October 14–17, 1987.
44. Bratton interview.
45. Ibid.
46. David Maraniss, *First in His Class* (New York: Simon & Schuster, 1995), 412.
47. Sam Bratton, telephone interview, February 15, 2010.
48. Susan May, telephone interview, November 25, 2009.
49. Kennedy, "Arkansas Teacher Testing," 9.
50. Clinton interview.
51. Kennedy, "Arkansas Teacher Testing," 11.
52. *Phil Donahue Show,* May 1, 1985; *Arkansas Gazette,* May 2, 1985, 1A.
53. John Walker, on the *Phil Donahue Show,* May 1, 1985.
54. Kennedy, "Arkansas Teacher Testing," 9.
55. *Arkansas Gazette,* June 27, 1985, p. 1A
56. Charles Moore, quoted in *Arkansas Gazette,* July 8, 1985, 1A.
57. Clinton interview.
58. *Lake View School District No. 25 of Phillips County v. Huckabee,* 351 Ark. 31, 91 S.W.3d 472 (Arkansas Supreme Court, November 21, 2002).

Jim Guy Tucker

1. Jim Guy Tucker, quoted in *Arkansas Gazette,* December 13, 1992, 1A.
2. Jim Guy Tucker, interview with author, November 10, 2009, Little Rock, AR.
3. *Arkansas Gazette,* December 2, 1992, 1A.
4. Tucker interview.
5. Parnell-Tucker Feud, in Kenneth Bridges's *The Encyclopedia of Arkansas History and Culture* (Little Rock, AR: Butler Center for Arkansas Studies, 2009).
6. Jim Guy Tucker, *Arkansas Men at War* (Little Rock, AR: Pioneer Press, 1968).
7. Tucker interview.
8. Richard Weiss, interview with author, November 17, 2009, Little Rock, AR.
9. Dent Gitchel interview with author, November 6, 2009, Little Rock, AR.
10. *Arkansas Gazette,* December 5, 1992, 14A.
11. *Arkansas Gazette,* December 9, 1992, 1A.
12. Bobby Hogue, interview with author, November 16, 2009, Little Rock, AR.
13. Bynum Gibson, telephone interview with author, November 16, 2009.
14. H. L. Mencken, "The Divine Afflatus," *New York Evening Mail,* November 16, 1917.
15. Hogue interview.
16. *Arkansas Gazette,* December 5, 1992, 1A.
17. Craig Rains, quoted in *Arkansas Gazette,* December 9, 1992, 16A.
18. *Arkansas Gazette,* December 6, 1992, 20A.
19. Ibid., December 14, 1992, 5B.
20. Tucker, quoted in ibid.
21. Ibid., December 15, 1992, 5B.
22. *Arkansas Gazette,* December 16, 1992, 5D.
23. Ibid., December 19, 1992, 11A.
24. Earnest Cunningham, quoted in ibid.
25. Stanley Russ, quoted in *Arkansas Gazette,* December 17, 1992, 5B.
26. *Arkansas Gazette,* December 19, 1992, 11A.
27. Jodie Mahony, quoted in ibid.
28. Hogue interview.
29. *Arkansas Gazette,* July 16, 1996, 7A.
30. Tucker, quoted in ibid.
31. *Arkansas Gazette,* July 17, 1996, 9A.
32. Gibson telephone interview.
33. Tucker, quoted in *Arkansas Gazette,* July 17, 1996, 8A.
34. Stanley Russ, quoted in *Arkansas Gazette,* July 17, 1996, 9A.

Mike Huckabee

1. *Lake View School District No. 25 of Phillips County v. Huckabee,* 351 Ark. 31, 91 S. W. 3d 472 (Arkansas Supreme Court, November 21, 2002).
2. Jim Argue, interview with author, July 16, 2009, Little Rock, AR.

3. Michael Dougan, "The Origins and Future of Public Education in Arkansas," Education Position paper prepared for state senator Steven Bryles, 2003 (used as a source for facts in the ensuing paragraphs).

4. Dougan, "Public Education," 5.

5. *Dupree v. Alma School District No. 30*, 279 Ark. 340, 651 S. W. 2d 90 (Arkansas Supreme Court, May 31, 1983).

6. Mike Huckabee, *Quit Digging Your Grave with a Knife and Fork* (New York: Center Street, Time Warner Book Group, 2005).

7. Mike Huckabee, State of the State Address, January 14, 2003.

8. Ibid.

9. Ibid.

10. Mike Huckabee, interview with author, September 29, 2009, North Little Rock, AR.

11. Rex Nelson, interview with author, October 13, 2009, Little Rock, AR.

12. Argue interview.

13. Huckabee interview.

14. Ibid.

15. Ibid.

16. Ibid.

17. Jim Argue, telephone interview with author, December 11, 2009.

18. Huckabee interview.

19. Ibid.

20. Act 60 of Second Extraordinary Session of 2003, Acts of Arkansas.

21. Public School Districts, Arkansas Department of Education, December 4, 2009.

22. Nelson interview.

23. Huckabee interview.

24. Ray Simon, telephone interview with author, October 20, 2009.

25. Smart Start and Smart Step were initiatives by the Arkansas Department of Education to assure student improvement and achievement in reading and math. Smart Start focused on kindergarten through fourth grade, beginning in 1998. Smart Step focused on grades five through eight. The programs gave teachers additional materials and assistance to achieve grade-level goals. Progress was tracked through Benchmark exams. Act 999 of 1999 established the Arkansas Comprehensive Testing, Assessment, and Accountability Programs, which supported the Smart Start initiative and have since been updated.

26. Simon interview.

27. Huckabee interview.

28. Simon interview.